I0133230

THE EFFECT OF TEACHERS' TRAITS ON

JOB SATISFACTION

A Dissertation Presented to the
Faculty of the College of Education
University of Houston

In Partial Fulfillment
of the Requirements for the Degree

Doctor of Education

by

Jessica deValentino

May, 2005

ACKNOWLEDGEMENT

I would like to thank my friends and family for their continued support and belief in me throughout my life. I am grateful that God thought so much of me to bless me with the two best grandparents that have ever and will ever live, Kay and Jesse Howe. Their limitless love, support, and generosity helped formed the person that I am today. I would like to thank my mother and father, Tracy and Donnie for their continued support throughout my life. I would like to thank my son, Mattiece for understanding when I was studying and working and not as fun as I should have been.

I am extremely appreciative to the wonderful professors that have guided me through this process. I would like to thank Dr. Alexander for his methodological expertise not only during my doctoral studies, but also during my undergraduate studies. I would like to thank Dr. Hooker for his support, guidance, and humor throughout the years. I would like to thank Dr. Liberman for his knowledge, support, and guidance. I would like to thank Dr. Phillips for her direction, expertise, and support. And last, but not least, I would like to thank Dr. Zou for her wisdom, support, and encouragement.

I would like to thank God for bringing each of these wonderful individuals into my life and providing me with the strength, ability, endurance, and patience to finish this program.

THE EFFECT OF TEACHERS' TRAITS ON

JOB SATISFACTION

An Abstract
of
A Dissertation Presented to the
Faculty of the College of Education
University of Houston

In Partial Fulfillment
of the Requirements for the Degree

Doctor of Education

by

Jessica deValentino

May, 2005

deValentino, Jessica "The Effect of Teachers' Traits on Job Satisfaction." Unpublished Doctor of Education Dissertation. University of Houston, May, 2005.

Abstract

The purpose of this study is to describe the extent to which selected factors are predictive of teachers' job satisfaction. This was accomplished through the collection and analysis of multiple measures of teachers' traits. The criterion variable was teachers' perceived job satisfaction. The predictor variables were teachers' perceived involvement and participation, teachers' perceived motivation, grade level of instruction, stipend recipient, and years of teaching experience.

The population for this study was comprised of teachers from the Houston Independent School District. Permission was granted by the University of Houston's Committee for the Protection of Human Subjects and the Houston Independent School District's Research and Accountability Department. The study proposed three research questions: (1) To what extent can teachers' traits (i.e. teachers' perceived job involvement, teachers' perceived motivation, grade level of instruction, stipend recipient, and years of teaching experience) predict their job satisfaction? (2) Of the traits (i.e. teachers' perceived job involvement, teachers' perceived motivation, grade level of instruction, stipend recipient, and years of teaching experience) which is the best predictor of the job satisfaction of teachers? (3) To what extent do teachers' perceived traits predict job satisfaction over and above their actual traits (years of teaching experience, stipend recipient, and grade level of instruction)?

Multiple regression analyses were utilized to interpret the data. The results of the data analysis supported the first research hypothesis, there was a statistically significant combined effect on the relationship between teachers' traits (as measures of teachers' perceived job involvement, teachers' perceived motivation, grade level of instruction, stipend recipient, and years of teaching experience) and their job satisfaction, $R^2 = .32$, adjusted $R^2 = .24$, $F (5, 46) = 4.34$ $p = .003$.

The second research hypothesis stated measures of teachers' perceived motivation have the highest correlation with teachers' perceived job satisfaction. The results of the data analysis did not support the hypothesis. The correlation between the measures of teachers' perceived involvement and participation, and teachers' perceived job satisfaction was found to be the highest, $r = .50$, $p < .001$.

The third research hypothesis stated measures of teachers' perceived traits will be statistically greater than their actual traits. The results of the data analysis supported the hypothesis, $R^2 = .258$, adjusted $R^2 = .228$, $F (2, 49) = .8.52$, $p < .001$. The measures of the actual traits did not significantly predict over and above the perceived traits, R^2 change = .06, $F (3, 46) = 1.41$, $p = .252$.

Utilizing the results that were generated from this study may help future school reformers plan initiatives that may improve teachers' job satisfaction, and thereby facilitate the academic progression of students.

TABLE OF CONTENTS

LIST OF TABLES

CHAPTER ONE

Introduction

The field of education has experienced a myriad of reform efforts in attempt to improve the overall quality of education in regards to instruction, policies, and procedures for students and teachers (Spillane, 1999). There may be a way to alleviate some of the problems and thereby increase the job satisfaction of teachers. Many teachers participate in a form of the suggested solution, however it's full capacity has yet to be realized. The solution may be a form of professional development known as professional learning communities. Purcell states, "More commonly, a professional development program is defined as including all those activities that help employees do their work better and gain greater satisfaction" (1987, p. 3).

More information is available now than at any other time and with each day more advancements are made in many academic areas. The field of education is rapidly changing and growing (Guskey, 2000). It is important for teachers to receive on-going training to keep abreast of new information (Speck & Knipe, 2001). In professional development, teachers are given information to enhance their teaching styles to better meet the needs of students (Guskey, 2000).

Educational researchers are making enormous advancements in understanding the learning process of students and increasing students' achievement (Guskey, 2000). Professional development is important because in the absence of considerable and effective professional developments many teachers will use the teaching strategies utilized when they were in school or out-dated strategies, with which they are most comfortable (Sparks & Hirsh, 1999).

Professional development must be implemented continually to educate teachers and to increase student performance (Speck & Knipe, 2001). Almost all improvements in education are associated with the implementation of professional development (Guskey, 2000). The U.S. Government has observed the importance and the need for professional development. In 1994, legislation passed a reform to increase financial support for professional development (Professional Development Today, 1996). In 1996, a report by the National Commission of Teaching & America's Future (NCTAF) stated a portion of five billion dollars of government money was allocated for professional development (Ballinger, 2000).

Guskey (2000) states, "Professional development is defined as those processes and activities designed to enhance the professional knowledge, skills, and attitudes of educators to improve the learning of students" (p. 16). In addition, Guskey informs, "Every proposal for educational reform and every plan for school improvement emphasizes the need for high-quality professional development" (2000, p. 3). Moreover, in order to increase student achievement, it is necessary to provide and improve professional development activities of teachers (Speck & Knipe, 2001). "School improvement specialists generally recommend that a school district devotes at least 10 percent of its operating budget to staff development and that teachers devote at least 25 percent of their work time to personal learning" (NSDC, p. 1). Sparks and Hirsch state, "the typical school spends only 0.05 percent of its budget on raising the abilities of its staff while the typical private-sector company spends nearly four times as much" (Sparks & Hirsch, 1999). Sparks and Hirsh (1999) report from a study by Greenwald, Hedges, and Laine that, "Student achievement goes up more for every $500 spent on increasing teacher professional training than for spending the same amount on raising teacher salaries or reducing class sizes" (p. 5).

When teachers' needs are met, they are more capable of effectively meeting all of the demands of the job (Gaziel, 1993). A part of the solution may be investigating the variables that affect job satisfaction. According to Bredson and Scribner, "...most teachers are intrinsically motivated to update their skills, to grow professionally, and to remain in the field of teaching through the belief they are having a positive effect on their students' learning and social growth" (2000, p. 64). Therefore, it can be derived that teachers want to increase their skills and to be more proficient professionals to help students reach their learning objectives and goals. Moreover, the literature conveys there is a relationship between the knowledge of teachers and student achievement (NSDC, p. 3).

Professional development is especially important to new teachers. New teachers are faced with the immense responsibilities of learning a myriad of components involved in teaching and assisting students in reaching the state standards of academic achievement. New teachers need the resources given in professional development activities to build their repertoire of instructional skills (Johnson & Kardos, 2002).

Professional development is a very important process, which increases teachers' knowledge of instructing and understanding of students' styles of learning. A key component in the success of new programs or reforms is professional development (Guskey, 2000). Although extremely important, many educators are not interested in professional development, and they state that professional development is not related to their daily tasks of instructing (Guskey, 2000).

Schools and school districts frequently neglect teachers in the planning process. The disregard approach to employee management emerged around the turn of the 20th century. Many industries implemented a simplistic system in attempt to specialize jobs and to improve the quality of products. This cookie cutter scheme was successful for a time when workers were uneducated and undemanding. In the 1950's, literature from Argyris, Likert, and McGregor began to appear concerning the blandness of the design of jobs. These theorists thought the assembly line design would reduce employees' motivation, productivity, and the quality of the products (Lawler, 1986).

Today's workforce is more educated and more demanding. They display an unwillingness to comply blindly with supervisors and organizational leaders. There is evidence that supports employees are less comfortable with autocratic work systems that do not provide an opportunity for employee involvement (Lawler, 1986). Employees have increased expectations for their employment. Employees want their careers to motivate and satisfy them (Mohrman, 1994). Research supports that many employees want to be involved with the inter-workings of their employment organization (Lawler, 1986).

Over the next ten years, the field of education will need to attract and sustain a good working relationship with over two million new teachers (Johnson, Liu, Kaufmann Kardos, & Peske; 2001). A good working relationship is important because the results from a study found that 20% of teachers leave the field of education within their first four years of teaching (Johnson, 2001).

The tribulations teachers experience manifest into a variety of negative outcomes such as: attrition, stress, burnout, shortage, and entrapment. School reformers have identified parts of programs, roles, structures, and processes essential to successful reform efforts, however the magical formula for the ideal school reform has not become apparent (Spillane, Henderson & Diamond; 2004). A study done by Corwin (2001) states, "…an overwhelming 61% of teachers indicated their schools were in the midst of a decline in teacher morale" (p. 18). Only attending to the instructional development needs of teachers leaves many other areas of need neglected (Turbowitz & Longo, 1997). Teachers need a forum to discuss the various challenges and ideas involving teaching (Johnson & Kardos, 2002; Dinham, 1994).

Need for the Study

A significant goal of education is to educate students, which with the surmounting plights of students, is an ever changing and difficult task. Of course, there may be employees that do not want to be involved, and research studies show that these employees are typically less committed and less satisfied with their work (Wu & Short, 1996). If reform efforts are to be successful, teachers must work outside of their realm of comfort and complacency, and reach the height of their instructional ability. Instead of professional developments with simple presentations, teachers need to engage in a form of professional development that encourages development through meaningful exchanges to meet the academic needs of students (Harris, 2003).

Many education reformers have devised massive plans for the curriculum and policies of schools; however, without the drive and support of teachers, their plans are futile (Spillane, 1999). The results of studies suggest "changes designed with little involvement of those destined to use them are rarely successful" therefore, teachers need to participate and have an active role in reform efforts (Mulford & Silins, 2003, p. 191).

The aim of professional development is to increase student learning through instructional strategies and methods presented to teachers. Teachers may spend several hours listening to a presenter and leave with a couple of teaching tips (Professional Development Today, 1995) and this is not enough to make a significant impact on students' achievement.

> The image and focus of professional development needs to be altered to increase the level of interest to teachers and ultimately provide a positive impact on student achievement. Schools that are able to offer their teachers a safe, pleasant, and supportive environment … are better able to attract and retain good teachers and motivate them to do their best (Choy, 1996, p. 1).

Statement of the Problem

The nation is clamoring for noteworthy developments in school reforms. In many schools there is a top-down management approach that leaves much to be desired in regards to true involvement efforts (Lambert, 2002). Teachers experience many difficulties working in the field of education. Many school districts are struggling with the shortage of teachers (Bentacourt-Smith, Iman, & Marlow; 1994). Ballinger reports, "Despite increasing numbers of teachers reaching retirement age, experts believe it is teacher retention that will be the biggest factor in what many are predicting will be a serious teacher shortage" (2000, p. 1). Ballinger states that the problem is not the insufficient quantity of certified teachers, it is the attrition rate. National estimates report that 30 to 50% of all new teachers will leave the field of teaching within their first three to five years. The literature and large teacher attrition rate suggest that teachers experience a lack of job satisfaction, which leads to the discontinuation of their employment in the field of education (Ballinger, 2000).

Moreover, when low job satisfaction occurs, high turnover rates usually follow. There are numerous problematic issues associated with high turnover rates, such as the cost of recruiting, processing of new hires, and training. These unpleasant costs make it important to try to minimize turnover rates as much as possible (Ingersoll, 1999). "Researchers report that employee turnover can cost anywhere from 5 to 25 times an employee's salary due to factors such as cost incurred with training, recruiting, low performance, and overstaffing to prevent an insufficient workforce" (Lawler, 1986, p. 86).

Administrators and school reformers may have at one time been in the classroom, but times and situations change. Teachers have current first hand knowledge on the current state and needs of the students in their classrooms. However, their involvement in the planning process is reportedly very limited. Education reformers, and other individuals in leadership roles with the privilege to make significant changes are very interested in implementing the next best practice or reform at their school or schools. Many times the plans are fully created, and at the final stage of implementation, the plans are presented to teachers. With convincing arguments, many teachers are ready to proceed, however there is something missing, which is the teachers' job involvement and motivation, which may influence their job satisfaction (Johnson & Landman, 2000). The research states that it is very important to elicit and involve employees if any vision or strategy is to be realized (Leach, Wall, & Jackson, 2003). Johnston, Griffeth, Burton, and

Carson, (1993) report that employees with low motivation tend to withdraw from the company.

There are teachers who will try any idea and reform plan that is available. Teachers may be driven by the hope of changing and improving the lives of children through education or they may simply work to their highest capacity with any task. The results from a study by Bozionelos (2004) suggest that there are certain characteristics associated with job involvement, which may be an influencing factor in the drive of some good teachers. However, there are the teachers that are not reached. They simply go through the motions of plan implementation, but withhold the effort that is essential to success.

There are many teachers exiting the field of education and others who are not content working in the field of education who may follow. When teachers exit the field of education they take with them their knowledge of students' learning styles, instructional techniques, professional development training, and the knowledge of the system of education. Students thereby lose the benefit of having teachers with an educational background and are left with new inexperienced teachers (Ingersoll, 1999).

There are inadequacies in the fulfillment of teachers' needs in the field of education. The large teacher attrition rate suggests there may be issues concerning the lack of job satisfaction teachers experience, which leads to the discontinuation of their employment in the field of education. Although one of the primary goals of education is to meet the educational needs of the students, teachers must have their needs met as well. Escaping the bureaucracy, imposed policies, and instructional infringements of the traditional school organization is clearly a factor from the reporting of Keller (1997) who stated that 10,000 teachers in Massachusetts applied for 400 positions in the first charter school of the state for the opportunity to work with less constraints and more instructional freedom (Johnson & Landman, 2000).

Over the last 25 years, there has been an increase in job research, suggesting dissatisfaction with a job may lead to employee withdrawal (Hom, Caranikis-Wilker, Prussia, & Griffeth, 1992; Hom & Griffeth, 1995; Hom & Kinicki, 2001). "Contrary to many employers' perceptions, employees of all generations are becoming less likely to 'job hop,'" according to the study reported by Community Banker (2001, p. 42). In addition, more than 75 % of employees state it is important for them to engage in a long-term employment commitment with a company (Community Banker, 2001). Therefore, helping employees to achieve job satisfaction would be a beneficial endeavor.

Purpose of the Study

The purpose of this study was to describe the extent to which teachers' traits (i.e. perceived job involvement, perceived motivation, level of instruction, stipend recipient, and years of teaching experience) were able to predict their job satisfaction. The results of the study may assist school administrators and school reformers in making more informed decisions concerning teachers in future plans and initiatives, and thereby facilitate endeavors to increase student achievement.

There has been a significant amount of research done in the field of psychology and business concerning the variables of job involvement, motivation, and job satisfaction. This study went further than previous research to describe the individual and combined effect of multiple factors on teachers' job satisfaction. This study may provide educational leaders and reformers with important information that may significantly impact future reform efforts and school initiatives, and thereby improve student instruction.

Teachers are not expected to remain in the same position or in a school for their entire careers. However, teachers should experience job satisfaction with their profession and should be positive additions to their employment organization for the good of the individuals that come into contact with the organization such as the students, colleagues, parents, school leaders, and the community. Perhaps through understanding the effect of multiple variables on the job satisfaction of teachers there may be positive enhancements in future reform efforts and initiatives.

Research Questions

The less than successful implementation of reform efforts and teachers' lack of job satisfaction are a hindrance to the academic achievement of students. Significant changes are needed in reform efforts and strategies in concern to teachers. Survey research methods were used to gather data concerning teachers' self-reported traits and perceptions. Multiple linear regression and correlation analyses were performed on the data to determine the effect of the variables on job satisfaction. The results of the study may suggest new information to assist in the development of positive reforms regarding teachers.

1. To what extent can teachers' traits (i.e. perceived job involvement, perceived motivation, level of instruction, stipend recipient, and years of teaching experience) predict the job satisfaction of teachers?

2. Of the predictor variables (i.e. perceived job involvement, perceived motivation, level of instruction, stipend recipient, and years of teaching experience) which is the best predictor of the job satisfaction of teachers?

3. To what extent do teachers' perceived traits (teacher involvement and participation, and motivation) predict job satisfaction over and above their actual traits (level of instruction, stipend recipient, and years of teaching experience)?

Research Hypotheses

1. There is a statistically significant combined effect in the relationship between teachers' traits (as measures of perceived job involvement, perceived motivation, level of instruction, stipend recipient, and years of teaching experience) and the job satisfaction of teachers.

2. The measures of teachers' perceived motivation have the highest correlation with the job satisfaction of teachers.

3. The measures of teachers' perceived traits will be statistically greater than the actual traits of the teachers.

Definition of Terms

Professional Development –

Orlich (1988) reports,

> Staff development describes the totality of the activity used in a formal organization to improve the education, training skills, attitudes, or personal attributes of all members of a specific organization. Staff development denotes the expansion, enhancement, and improvement of the totality of human potential. In-service education denotes projects and processes which are based on identified needs, planned and designed for a specific group of individuals in a school district, having a specific set of learning objectives or activities and are designed to extend, add or improve immediate job-oriented skills, competencies or knowledge (p.7).

Stipend – compensation paid to a teacher in addition to his or her base salary for fulfilling requirements, including but not limited to: (a) teaching a specialized subject (i.e. bilingual, special education), (b) teaching a critical need area (i.e. math, science), (c) participating in a committee, or (d) sponsoring / coaching a sport or a club.

CHAPTER TWO

Review of Literature

Introduction

The purpose of this study was to describe the extent to which teachers' traits, (perceived job involvement, perceived motivation, level of instruction, stipend recipient, and years of teaching experience) predict the job satisfaction of teachers. There is a large amount of information available concerning job satisfaction and work related issues. However, very few studies focus on the extent to which teachers' traits predict job satisfaction. Business, education, and psychology research was used to develop the review of literature. Throughout the literature review there are references made about teachers and employees. Although, at many times the reference of the term "employees" is drawn from business and psychology related literature, teachers are indeed employees, in one of the largest industries, and it is reasonable to fathom that many of the promising strategies used with employees of other industries, may have promising effects with teachers. The first section focuses on the negative outcomes of teaching. The following sections focus on the factors that are associated with job satisfaction, the first of which is professional development. Next is professional learning communities, which is a form of professional development and the framework of this study. Thereafter is motivation. In addition to motivation, the review of literature elaborates on the different theoretical approaches to motivation that explain behavior, which also relates to job satisfaction. Thereafter, the review of the literature continues with findings concerning the multi-facets of job involvement. Next is a review of compensation. The chapter concludes with a summary.

Negative Outcomes of Teaching

As relayed in the preceding literature, job satisfaction is an essential component of the working relationship. There are several significant negative outcomes that occur when teachers experience a lack of job satisfaction in the field of education, which are stress, burnout, entrapment, absenteeism, and attrition (Hammonds & Onikama, 1997). These problems have many adverse effects to the entire field of education. That is why it is imperative that measures are taken to gain a greater understanding of the aspects that affect job satisfaction to make the needed improvements. The following literature relays the ominous conditions that teachers may endure as a result of deficits in the area of job satisfaction.

"Stress can affect teachers' job satisfaction and their effectiveness with pupils" (Abel & Sewell, 1999, p. 287). Stress causes a downfall in numerous areas such as energy, quality of teaching, and working relationships (Abel & Sewell, 1999). Researchers state that it is important to deal with the problems associated with stress because prolonged stress erodes many coping resources, which eventually leads to burnout (Abel & Sewell, 1999). In addition, many people who experience stress often alleviate their stress through negative means such as alcohol consumption or drug abuse (Hunter, 1989). In addition, stress may inhibit the ability of a teacher to provide quality instruction to students (Gaziel, 1993).

Webster's (1988) defines burnout as "exhaustion of physical; or emotional strength." Teacher burnout is an important issue in the field of education that many researchers have studied and tried to remedy (Townsend, 1992). There are many similarities between stress and burnout. However, burnout is a progressed state of stress.

Therefore, when teachers continually experience a high level of stress, burnout occurs. Researchers explain that burnout is comprised of many negative variables, which teachers incur while working, such as exhaustion, depersonalization, and reduced personal accomplishment (Abel & Sewell, 1999). From the literature, it is plausible to consider that providing teachers with a forum at work where they can flourish may increase their satisfaction (DuFour, et. al, 2002).

Depersonalization is known to cause negative feelings to be projected toward students due to the lack of emotional resources to effectively deal with stress (Abel & Sewell, 1999). Teacher burnout may be ignited from "high levels of prolonged stress related to inordinate time demands, inadequate collegial relationships, large class size, lack of resources, isolation, role ambiguity, limited promotional opportunities, lack of support and involvement in decision-making, and student behavioral problems" (Abel & Sewell, 1999, p. 298).

Stress and burnout may produce absenteeism in teachers. When a teacher experiences stress or becomes burnt out, he or she may feel as though he or she cannot continue. In some cases, teachers fall into the pattern of not attending work on a regular basis (Scott & Wimbush, 1992). In their study, Scott & Wimbush (1992) found teacher absenteeism creates setbacks in the educational system. The study, which investigated absenteeism, was conducted in three urban school districts. The researchers found that approximately $500 million per year of the combined school districts' budgets was utilized to fund the cost associated with the absences of teachers. When a teacher is absent, many costs result such as: (a) the teachers' salary, (b) the wage of substitute teachers, and (c) the administrative cost in terms of the time required to complete all of the needed transactions with a teacher's absence.

With the progression of dissatisfaction, teachers search for new professions, and the system of education experiences teacher attrition. Shann, reports, "According to some estimates, 50% of beginning teachers leave the profession within five years" (2001, p. 67). Some of the most significant rates of attrition can be observed in urban school districts (Shann, 2001). Many of the reasons given by teachers for attrition are "the lack of administrative, collegial, and parental support and insufficient involvement in decision-making" (Shann, 2001, p. 67). Therefore, professional learning communities may be a useful resource in assisting teachers in combating negative factors (DuFour, 2002).

A study by Dworkin (1987) reports that although teachers experience burnout and a lack of job satisfaction, there are a significant number of teachers who will remain in the field of teaching. The teachers who remain in the field of teaching may be suffering from feelings of entrapment. Entrapment may be described as the point when a teacher no longer wants to remain in the field of teaching; but remains because of many facets that may affect a teacher if he or she leaves. Some of the grim situations teachers may try to avoid are the inability to find work in a different field and the loss of optimal retirement options (Dworkin, 1987). "The desire to quit teaching, a key element in entrapment, can be reduced when burnout levels are lowered by increasing teachers' feelings of satisfaction" (Hunter, 1989 p. 18).

Professional Development

For teachers there are numerous terms used interchangeably to describe professional development such as: in-service training, professional growth, staff development, continuing education, on-the-job training, organization development, in-service teacher education, continued professional development, and in-service education (Orlich, 1988). Orlich (1989) states, the beginning of in-service training occurred approximately a century ago. Kershaw (1995) reports, the first in-services were not created for professional growth, rather as a form of the present day alternative certification programs. Professional developments typically occur within a short period of time, from one day to a week. Tyler (1971) informs, the information of in-service trainings is generally remedial and pertinent to classroom applications.

Tyler (1971) affirms, at the end of the Eight-Year Study, which began in 1933, significant progress was achieved concerning professional development. The focus of professional developments shifted from remedial education to in-services of innovative applications of educational topics, which were of greater interest to teachers.

As time has progressed, others have noticed the importance for professional development. In 1969, the National Staff Development Council (NSDC) was created. The NSDC is the largest non-profit professional association devoted to increased student achievement through the implementation of professional development. In addition, the National Staff Development Council has developed many standards to maintain the quality and effectiveness of professional development (Guskey, 2000).

Professional development is important for numerous reasons. Professional development has positive effects on the lives of teachers and students by assisting in teachers professional development, and altering teachers' beliefs, values, and approaches to teaching students (Guskey, 1985; Hawthorne, 1983; Purcell, 1987). Professional development gives teachers an opportunity to increase their base of knowledge and resources, and assists them in remaining abreast of the latest information in their field (Howey, 1985; Purcell, 1987). Teachers need to have continual training to update their skills (Sparks & Hirsh, 1999), and when teachers' needs are met, they are more capable of effectively meeting all of the demands of the job (Community Banker, 2001).

Professional development delivers many great instructional ideas and strategies to teachers such as ideas on how to keep students motivated and stimulated. There are other uses for professional development such as increasing staff camaraderie, "…unifying and motivating the staff, working towards a common goal, clarifying problems, suggesting solutions," and introducing and implementing new ideas and procedures (Purcell, 1987, p. 10). Purcell states, professional development is a multifaceted operation including, but not limited to the areas of "improving skills, implementing curricular procedures, expanding subject matter knowledge, making and organizing instruction, and increasing personnel effectiveness" (Dale, 1983; Solo, 1985; Purcell 1997, p. 4).

Problems

Professional development provides teachers with valuable information and resources, however there are many problems associated with traditional professional development models. Some of the problems include, but are not limited to the lack of planning of professional development presentation, the lack of continued support for the professional development activity, the lack of teachers' interest in the information presented, and the lack of diversity in themes (Boyd, 1997).

Teachers have a limited part in the planning of professional development (Boyd, 1993). Administrators' ability to force teachers to accept and implement change in many circumstances is limited (Boyd, 1993). Boyd states, "Jones and Lowe (1990) propose a 'bottom-up' approach whereby programs are planned and implemented by those teachers affected by them" (1993, p. 6). In addition, when teachers take part in the planning process of professional development activities they can choose the themes that most interest them.

Professional development activities usually give extensive information on new methods applicable to teaching styles or teachers' resources. Although extensive in quantity, many professional development activities usually come in the form of one-shot stops (Lauro, 1995). Shortly thereafter the professional development activities are quickly abandoned for the latest ideas due to different circumstances such as lack of commitment from the staff, lack of funds, or impatience (Lauro, 1995). The constant inundation of innovative methods presented in professional development activities makes it difficult for teachers to gain a thorough understanding of the information presented, and to perfect or modify teaching strategies for optimal results to student achievement. Often, even when teachers are fond of the new instructional strategies, the presenters and support are nowhere to be found, which eventually causes the demise of the implemented strategies (Boyd, 1993). Teachers need time to reflect on the information presented and to integrate the information into their plans, lessons, and curriculum (Harris, 2003).

Professional development activities generally focus on strategies and methods for teachers to utilize when instructing students. Many of the activities addressed in professional development are not related or continuous. Teachers are expected to combine all of the different activities, methods, and strategies to make meaningful, instructional lessons for students, which can be a difficult and arduous task, especially for new teachers (Hixson & Tinzmann, 1990; Johnson & Kardos, 2002).

Professional development activities are not one size fits all. Although it may be cost effective to implement one professional development activity across the school, the activities may not be customized enough to stimulate the interest of all the teachers. Teachers practice the art of teaching with various strengths, weaknesses, and years of experience. In addition, new and veteran teachers may need different combinations of resources, ideas, mentoring and personal and professional development (Evertson, 1986; Rubin, 1978; Purcell, 1987). Although instructional strategies are very important factors in teaching students, they are not the only area that may increase the developmental growth of teachers. Neglecting areas of teachers' needs facilitates the growth of problems and decreases teachers' morale.

Overall, teachers are not enthusiastic and do not demonstrate a genuine interest in professional development (Brimm and Tollett, 1974). Lambert (1989) states, most professional development endeavors are futile and do not provide effective results. Brimm and Tollett (1974) conducted a research study in Tennessee with teachers concerning their opinions of in-service training. A major concern of the teachers was the lack of opportunity to actively participate in the selection of information presented during professional development. Furthermore, many teachers felt previous professional developments were not beneficial to their needs. Moreover, over half of the teachers stated they do not like to attend in-service training.

Boyd reports, "Educational leaders (administrators, school boards, policy makers) should know, if they do not already, that many teachers reject most typical staff developments or in-services with contempt and ridicule" (Ryan, 1987; Boyd, 1993, p. 1-2). In addition, some teachers have described professional developments as boring, repetitious, and a waste of time (Brimm and Tollett, 1974). Adults are often more pragmatic than theoretical and often tend to reject information when it is presented in an ambiguous or irrelevant theory (Caffarella, 1988; Boyd, 1993).

As the literature relays there are negative factors of professional development that contribute to teachers' low job satisfaction, which may inhibit their ability to be effective instructional providers. If implemented correctly, professional development can be a wonderful tool to better equip teachers to meet the demands of the students and schools. Therefore, it is important to assist teachers in engaging in meaningful activities that will not only enhance themselves, but the students (Strahan, 2002).

Solutions

For all of the good intentions in the concept of professional development there are various inadequacies that cause professional development activities to be less successful than intended. There are many problems associated with professional development, however professional development activities provide teachers with innovation information to stimulate their teaching style and avoid stagnation (Purcell, 1987). There is not a magical remedy to all the issues in education, however part of the solution may be found by broadening the scope of traditional professional development to innovative professional development activities that encourage increased teacher participation (DuFour, Guidice, Magee, Martin, & Zivkovic; 2002).

Many times the effectiveness of professional developments is assessed by the degree it was liked by the recipients (Brimm and Tollett, 1974). It is paramount to determine why many teachers do not like and are not interested in professional development (Brimm and Tollett, 1974). Not only must teachers have an intrinsic desire to incorporate new skills into their teaching style, but they must also continuously reflect, exchange ideas, and develop innovative ways to improve students' academic achievement (Purcell, 1987).

A study done by Chan, Gee, & Steiner states, "As a group happier employee companies have statistically significant better performance than a group of comparable companies in their industries" (2000, p. 47). An article in Community Banker stated, "Satisfied employees improve customer service and lower employee turnover" (Community Banker, 2001, p. 42). Therefore, by meeting the needs of teachers, benefits may follow such as higher job satisfaction and an increase student achievement.

Sparks (1999) states,

> Professional development, however, must be considerably different than those offered in the past, affecting not only the knowledge, attitudes, and practices of individual teachers, administrators and other school employees, but also the cultures and structures of the organizations in which those individuals belong p. 260

A more humanistic and or affective approach may be beneficial to implement into professional development. Boyd states, (as cited in Clark, Lotto, and Astuto, 1984) "they... observed that staff development must evolve beyond the isolated dimension of improving teaching skills and they... contend this can be accomplished by moving towards psychological support and personal reinforcement ..." (1993, p. 5). Humanistic refers not only to human condition, but the rights of individuals to make choices and decisions (Hesset, 1990; Boyd, 1993). Affective has been referred to as values, feelings, attitudes, emotions, and degree of acceptance or rejection (Hein, 1973; Boyd, 1993). "One possible approach to affective or humanistic staff development is to provide instruction and activities which fosters good mental and emotional health among teachers" (Boyd, 1993, p. 6). Boyd states, "A professional development program should focus on the problems of people throughout the organization and should consider the 'psychological needs of the staff'" (Thompson & Cooley, 1984, Boyd, 1993, p. 4). Teachers pontificating and exchanging strategies may build improved collegiate relationships, thereby providing teachers with a support system and facilitating school cohesiveness (Lafee, 2003).

Ho states, "Many professional development programs work on the assumption that providing teachers with prescribed skills and teaching recipes will produce better teachers, and the participants will accept, acquire, and adopt the skills and methods, introduced to them" (Biggs, 1989; Ramsden, 1992; Ho, 2000 p. 1). In order for professional development to be useful, teachers must implement the strategies and information presented. Teachers will only accept and implement new methods and strategies when they are properly motivated and willing (Boyd, 1993).

It is important to recognize all of the differentiated needs of a staff to align the individual goals of the teachers and the school (Clark and Siedman, 1980; Schambier, 1983). Professional development should be a collaborative process. Schambier states, "the failure of many staff development programs to negotiate their way through the plethora of needs, accounts for numerous, uncoordinated, and therefore, ineffective attempts to re-educate personnel" (2000, p. 5).

The key to professional development is to have good activities that meet not only the instructional and professional needs of the teachers, but allow teachers to reflect, internalize, and discuss the significance of the presentation. Parkay and Hoover state, "Staff development must focus on professional growth and learning — not on the elimination of imagined teacher deficiencies" (1986, p. 4).

"The most effective in-service activities are considered to be very personal experiences involving professionals, who as a result of their experience and training, have acquired strong feelings, individual styles, and commitments" (Bishop, 1976, p. 9). Schambier reports, "Fiske supports the concept of participant-centered in-service education and suggests that staff development may hold the key to higher morale among educators" (Schambier, 1983, p. 1).

Teachers should be actively involved in the selection and creation of professional development activities (Magestro, Stanford, & Blair, 2000). Teachers should feel they are included in the creation of professional development activities. The activities should be meaningful, and the activities should increase teachers' competence. When teachers are more involved in the creation of the professional development activities they may feel more ownership and may be more likely to buy into the activities, rather than if the activities are forced upon them (Boyd, 1993). Zeichner and Klehr (1999) state, professional development activities should center on issues teachers feel are important, contribute to their knowledge, and foster professional growth.

Teachers usually dread professional developments activities, therefore the image of professional development must change to increase the interest of teachers and eliminate the negative perceptions. The material presented in professional development activities has to be comprehendible, interesting, and relevant to the teachers, which may be accomplished by implementing innovative models of professional development. Therefore, from the literature just reviewed it is reasonable to believe that professional development is a forum that has yet to reach its full capacity, which appears to be very promising. Facilitating professional development to the point where teachers actively engage in thought provoking exchanges concerning the best line of action for improved student comprehension and achievement may be very rewarding and satisfying to teachers.

Professional Learning Communities

There have been a plethora of school models that were created to significantly improve the academic achievement of students (Jansen, 1995). Many researchers believe that reforms are cyclical, there are no perfect reforms, and the current reform will only survive until the next one arrives. Professional learning communities are one of the latest developments in education. Research suggests that professional learning communities increase the academic achievement of students by increasing teachers' roles in the planning and development process of instruction. The primary goal of professional learning communities is to achieve improved results in the academic achievement of students. The effectiveness of professional learning communities is not based on the efforts or the intentions of the teachers, but the results of teachers' instruction on student achievement (DuFour, Guidice, Magee, Martin, & Zivkovic; 2002).

Teachers are the mediums though which education flows. Therefore, in order to realize significant improvements in the academic achievement of students, there has to be significant differences in the preparation and practice of teachers. Teachers must be embodied with the knowledge, desire, motivation, and energy to make significant positive differences in the lives of students. This can be done by implementing the professional learning community model (Strahan, 2002).

In contrast to the traditional professional development model of the past, shared leadership models tap into the talents of the teachers (Lambert, 2002). The professional learning community model is built on three key components, which serve as the model for this study. The first component is ensuring the academic success of students (DuFour, et. al, 2002). Many teachers believe that the instructional and the learning process are complete after the presentation of a lesson to the students and the students complete an activity. However, as many educators are aware, each child is different, and frequently students do not master a lesson after an explanation and an activity. At this point, when students do not master objectives, teachers who participate in a professional learning community do not go on, they engage in meaningful exchanges with their colleagues to create instructional plans that promote the academic success of all students, without delaying the academic progression of the students that initially mastered the lesson (DuFour, et. al, 2002).

The second component in the model of a professional learning community is the establishment of a collaborative culture. The collaborative culture creates a synergy that allows ideas and learning to flourish. Professional learning communities encourage teachers to work collaboratively together. Teacher collaboration is one of the characteristics that has been consistently discovered in successful schools. Teacher collaboration may lead to improved student achievement (DuFour, et. al, 2002). There are many positive effects from teachers working collaboratively such as: shared ideas, the creation of new ideas, improved instructional strategies, the creation of a learning community, and social support among staff. Characteristics of successful schools include teachers taking part in risks for gains in students' academic achievement, learning from failed instructional implementation, and sharing ideas that lead to increased self-efficacy, higher goals, and improved student achievement (Strahan, 2002).

Teachers involved in professional learning communities participate in enriched forms of professional development, different from the traditional model of teaching, which the teacher works and prepares in isolation. Professional learning communities also demand a large commitment from the teachers. Teachers in professional learning communities need a significant amount of time for collaborating, planning, sharing, and learning to make significant strides in instruction. Teachers in professional learning communities engage in thought provoking ideas and strategizing that results in additional opportunities for student success (Strahan, 2002).

The last component of the professional learning community model is the focus on results. Professional learning communities base their effectiveness on the results that are produced from students' academic achievement. Professional learning communities are never ending journeys to facilitate in the academic development of students (DuFour, et. al, 2002). Researchers have found that successful professional learning communities emphasize that students' learning is the top priority and all teacher activity is focused on achieving this goal through collaborative efforts and an analysis of what is and is not effective (Leonard & Leonard, 2001).

Teachers experience several negative factors that erode their ability to effectively meet the needs of the students, however professional learning communities work to overcome the negative factors that teachers encounter such as burnout, lack of communication, restricted funds, isolation, and a missing support system (Leonard & Leonard, 2001). Schools that utilize professional learning communities create a culture that has a "collective efficacy". As teachers continue to share and develop ideas, a change transforms the culture and the climate of the school and there is the creation of a culture and a climate that is optimistic and encouraging. Teachers work cooperatively and collaboratively together, with an identified agenda created to enhance student achievement. The research has found that coordinated efforts of schools improve students' academic achievement (Strahan, 2002).

Frequently studies are done on why teachers leave the profession of teaching. Two of the top reasons that are given are a lack of satisfaction and a lack of support from the school. Frelow states, (as cited in Ballinger) "Teachers don't feel supported or valued" (Ballinger, 2000, p. 2). New teachers, as well as veteran teachers want to engage in meaningful dialogue that will facilitate their knowledge and skill as instructional providers (Johnson, & Kardos, 2002). Professional learning communities create an enriched culture through dialogue, introspection, collaboration, and assessment that is driven by the results of students' achievement and regulated by the shared leadership of teachers (Dufour, et. al 2002).

Professional learning communities utilize shared and distributed leadership styles. The success of professional learning communities has been attributed to teachers sharing and developing ideas and strategies (Farnsworth, 2002). Shared and distributed leadership styles encourage thoughts and ideas to be exchanged freely and openly to provide continuous improvement to the education of students (Lafee, 2003). Research has shown that student achievement is more likely to be improved when leadership is shared among the teachers within a school (Harris, 2003). "Many researchers have reported that effective schools have a collegial, familial environment that culminates in high teacher morale and satisfaction" (Zigarelli, 1996, p. 103).

To add significance and value to the leadership roles that are taken upon by teachers, a form of incentive or compensation must be provided to teachers for their leadership role to be truly effective (Harris, 2003). The beginning of compensation, a review of incentive plans, and a focus on some of the key benefits from utilizing additional forms of compensation are presented later in the review of literature. As it can be determined from the literature, professional learning communities and job satisfaction are clearly related. Professional learning communities encourage growth, provide a support system, and keep students' academic achievement the number one goal. Each of the components of professional learning communities may foster improved job satisfaction in teachers (Shann, 2001).

Job Satisfaction

Spector states, "Job satisfaction is the extent to which people like their jobs" (Spector, 1997; as cited in Hirschfield, 2000, p. 1). Job satisfaction produces good morale in employees, thus employees are able to work more efficiently and effectively (Hammond & Onikama, 1997). Job satisfaction is a very important component of the employment relationship (Hom & Kinicki, 2001). Satisfaction does not preclude that employees will perform well; however, it does signify that the employment relationship may continue (Lawler, 1986). When employees experience high job satisfaction, they are more likely to be productive (Community Banker, 2001). A study done by Chan, Gee, & Steiner (2000) states, "As a group happier employee companies have statistically significant better performance than a group of comparable companies in their industries" (p. 47). An article in Community Banker stated, "Satisfied employees improve customer service and lower employee turnover" (2001, p. 42).

Researchers suggest that commitment from the entire hierarchy of an organization is necessary to reach set goals. It is the personal commitment and investment of the employees that makes a profound difference on the outcome of goal attainment (Maehr, 1989; Rosenholtz, 1989; Wu & Short, 1996). Research has also found that a lack of commitment can appear as dissatisfaction in teachers, and this lack of satisfaction is unsatisfactory for the teachers, but detrimental to the academic development of students (Wu & Short, 1996).

When choosing the profession of teaching, teachers commit to learning the theory and practice of education, and they commit to assist in the education of students. Shortly after entering the field of education, many teachers become dissatisfied and unmotivated to continue. There are teachers who remain in the field of teaching long after they have lost their motivation to teach. The reason for many teachers continued employment in the field of education is not a desire to be a beneficial addition to the field of education, but as a return on their investment in their career. It is important to the academic success of students to have teachers who are motivated to put every effort forth (Herzberg, 1962). Job satisfaction produces good morale in employees, thus employees are able to work more efficiently and effectively (Hammond & Onikama, 1997).

Kim and Loadman (1994) conducted a study with over 2,000 participants and found "seven statistically significant predictors of job satisfaction: interactions with students, interactions with colleagues, professional challenges, professional autonomy, working conditions, salary, and opportunity for advancement" (Shann, 2001, p. 68). In a study by Hersey, employees were prompted to tell of a situation in their past performance, which they perceived themselves as being the most effective. In addition, to recalling a situation they felt they were most effective, employees also recalled being satisfied with their job as well (Herzberg, 1959). Moreover, when the respondents spoke of feelings of satisfaction, those feeling were associated with tasks, which they demonstrated successful work performances. The literature suggests that job satisfaction is essential to quality performance from employees. In regards to teachers, it may be reasonable to believe that job satisfaction influences the effort and instructional performance delivered to students. If teachers suffer from a lack job satisfaction, they may not possess the effort that is necessary to plan and implement good instructional strategies for students.

Motivation

Motivation appears to be one of the subcomponents of job satisfaction because the possibility of satisfaction is courtesy of motivation. At the beginning of every action there is motivation. Motivation describes the reasoning and desiring for the engagement of an individual in an activity. Motivation is influenced by a multitude of factors such as direction, persistence, and intensity (Fox, Moreira, & Sparkes, 2002; Van Knippenberg, 2000). When motivation is low, an outcome may not be as successful due to the insufficient desire to accomplish the goal. Therefore, it is vital to try to understand the factors that contribute to the motivation of teachers. Teachers need motivation to continue their pursuit of knowledge, to deliver interesting lessons, and inspire students to learn (Guskey, 2000).

At times, actions are influenced by the wants and the desires not within oneself, but by another. The desire of accomplishment is the essence of motivation. Participating in an activity that is integral with one's wants and desires leads to the realization of satisfaction. If a teacher desires to please and facilitate the plans of others, internalization of the plans should take place, and thereby become part of the teachers' motivation. Overall, teachers must be adequately motivated to meet expectations, and achieve goals. If one is highly motivated to do well at his or her job, he or she is more likely to experience high job satisfaction (Silver, 1982).

> For example, a teacher can more readily expect praise (favorable recognition), a sense of accomplishment (achievement), and the satisfaction of having learned something (growth possibility) as outcomes of investing efforts in teaching than he or she can expect a salary increase, more pleasant surroundings, and better supervision as outcomes of that effort. (Silver, 1982, p. 553)

The citation reveals that the expectancy of receiving recognition, the possibility of achievement, and the satisfaction of professional growth all serve as motivators for an individual. Motivation may be propelled by one's perceived benefit. In evaluating whether or not to complete an action the advantages and disadvantages are weighed.

After consideration, generally the variable perceived to be most advantageous is selected. The possibility of gaining a future benefit is a strong motivator for many individuals. In the event that a variable has no utility, many may not select the futile endeavor (Davis & Wilson, 2000).

> The motivation to perform an action is affected by the expectancy that a particular outcome can be achieved and by the desirability of that outcome in terms of its indirect effect based on past experiences, individuals make subjective estimates of their own abilities (expectancies) and the attainment of indirect outcomes (motivators and hygienes), which thus affect their motivation to perform future actions. (Silver, 1982, p. 553)

Motivation is a key component in committing employees to support and implement new endeavors and making improvements related to performance (Dessler, 1999; Lawler, 1986). Motivation enhances an employee's ingenuity, and thereafter they may create innovative strategies and ideas that will lead to an improved organization (Dessler, 1999).

Many researchers have expressed concern about extrinsic motivators, such as money, having a negative affect on the internal motivation of an individual (Herzberg, 1962). Kelley, Odden, Milanowski, and Heneman (2000) report that although many teachers may find bonuses desirable, they also function to increase internal motivation from the increased feelings of pride and self-worth after reaching a goal. It is vital to the success of any initiative to assess what employees may find satisfying before it is implemented as a reward. Anderman, Bleazer, and Smith (1998) found that satisfaction could be increased through a school culture that focuses on recognition and affiliation, both of which can be altered through motivation. Motivation can be credited in maintaining the interest and desire to accomplish a goal. Thereby when a goal is accomplished, it is more likely that job satisfaction will be achieved (Herzberg, 1962).

Scott and Wimbush (1991) report from their research, "Job satisfaction was the single most important factor affecting attendance motivation" (as cited in Hammond & Onikama, 1997, p. 3). In addition, teachers who experience satisfaction with their job tend to be absent less, which is important to the academic achievement and development of students. Studies suggest that employees who are motivated are more committed to finding success with their job. In regards to education, teachers are more likely to be better educational providers. Moreover, when teachers have goals to work toward they have the opportunity to experience job satisfaction. It may be argued that one does not have to have a goal or task that is associated with one's employment, to feel a sense of satisfaction; however, a unique sense of satisfaction is experienced when one reaches a specified goal (Herzberg, 1962).

Motivation helps battle problems that are encountered in daily work situations. Motivation may sustain one's desire to work productively to achieve goals, which may produce sentiments of satisfaction. Without motivation, employees may be ill equipped psychologically and void of an internal drive to perform well and please others. Therefore, it is important to maintain and enhance the motivation of all employees to enhance job satisfaction (Herzberg, 1962).

Job satisfaction is a measurement of morale in reference to employment. Research suggests that there is relationship that exists between job satisfaction and productivity. Productivity measures the output of an individual. Motivation drives behavior, which ultimately leads to a final product. Motivation is a special internalized force that is unique to each individual. Motivation is represented extrinsically through productivity, which is another of testament of why motivation is key to job satisfaction (Herzberg, 1962). Herzberg states that it is evident that job satisfaction is an integral part of motivation. He argues if all rewards were hygienically or extrinsically based then there would be no further desire for employees not to reach their full potential (Herzberg, 1962). From reviewing the literature, it is quite clear that satisfaction is a significant element of motivation.

Theory of Motivation

The connection between job satisfaction and motivation continues in motivational theory. The ability for one to be able to attain satisfaction is explained and embedded in motivational theory. There are many different motivational theories that attempt to explain the driving forces behind motivation and seek to improve relationships and outcomes (Dessler, 1999). Some of the motivational theories that will be reviewed are the hierarchy of needs theory, the hygiene-motivator theory, the expectancy theory, the equity theory, and the goal setting theory.

Many motivational theorists claim that behavior is influenced by the underlying tensions that cause an individual to initiate behaviors that will work to reduce tensions and thereby assist to reach a goal (Dessler, 1999). Motivational theorists contend that employees will be motivated to perform well when (a) rewards are associated to performance, (b) rewards are valued by the potential recipients, and (c) the goals are attainable (Lawler, 1986).

Maslow authored the hierarchy of needs theory, which elaborates on motivation (1959). Although not initiated by Maslow, the Hierarchy of needs theory has been organized into a triangular shape to represent the ascending tier of progressively challenging requisites to attain (Huizinga, 1970). The first rung of the hierarchy of needs theory concerns physiological needs, including the satiation of "food, water, sleep, shelter etc." (Huizinga, 1970, p. 21). The physiological needs are very strong and must be satiated before one can elevate to higher needs. Thereafter, there is the need to be safe and secure. These needs are called the safety needs. Safety needs include the need for "understandable, well-ordered, predictable situations" (Huizinga, 1970, p. 21). The social needs, also known as love and belonging needs are next. Social needs include "the need to love, to be loved, and to feel a close association with others" (Huizinga, 1970, p. 21). Self-esteem needs include the need or desire for a "stable, firmly based, usually high evaluation of oneself, for self-respect or self-esteem, and for the esteem of others" (Maslow, 1954, p. 90). The last level is self-actualization; at this stage an individual has substantially fulfilled his or her needs at the previous levels, and is ready to invest in his or her self to become completely fulfilled and reach the height of his or her capabilities. Many people never reach this stage, which is characterized by "the desire to become more and more what one is, to become everything that one is capable of becoming" (Maslow, 1954 p. 92).

Alderfer created an alternative theory based on Maslow's hierarchy of needs theory. Alderfer contends there are three essential needs that explain motivation, which are existence, relatedness, and growth. Existence encompasses the needs that are essential for human life. Relatedness deals with the need to feel an association and connection with others. Lastly, growth expresses a need for continuous progression for one to reach his or her fullest capabilities (Dessler, 1999).

From the fundamentals lying within Maslow's hierarchy of needs, Herzberg fashioned his own theory by separating the entire triangle of various human needs into two distinct areas, thereby creating the framework for the hygiene-motivator theory. "Dissastisfier factors essentially describe the environment and serve primarily to prevent job dissatisfaction, while having little effect on positive job attitudes, they have been named the hygiene factors" (Herzberg, 1962, p. 74). In order to alleviate dissatisfaction, the minimum factors must be present. The implementation of superfluous factors does not cause satisfaction. In addition, the pleasure that is experienced with the implementation of different external factors generally dissipates over time with a replaced interest for different external hygienic factors (Herzberg, 1959). Some of the factors that have been identified as dissatisfiers include, but are not limited to: "company policy and administration, supervision, interpersonal relations, working conditions, and salary" (Herzberg, 1962, p. 77).

The downfall of the hygiene factor is that the solution is only temporary. Therefore, one is seeking to be satisfied by avoiding factors that may cause dissatisfaction. Moreover, a hygienic environment, which is an environment that contains a plethora of pleasantries such as high and increasing salaries, lack of supervision, absence of policy, and an absence of an administration does not produce job satisfaction; however, there may be an absence of dissatisfaction. In order to obtain job satisfaction there must be the implementation of factors associated with motivators (Herzberg, 1962).

Motivators are intangible elements that function to proliferate the intrinsic goals and desires of individuals (Herzberg, 1962). "The 'satisfier' factors were named the motivators ...because they are effective in motivating... individuals to superior performance and effort" (Herzberg, 1962, p. 74). It is more practical to utilize motivator factors because they affect individuals intrinsically and permanently contrary to hygiene factors, which may continually and consistently require implementation and generally have short lasting effects (Herzberg, 1962). Motivators include, but are not limited to: "achievement, recognition, work itself, responsibility, and advancement" (Herzberg, 1962, p. 77).

It is important that teachers have high motivation because teachers with high motivation tend to experience high job satisfaction. Implementing motivators and demonstrating motivation are task factors. "To feel one has grown depends on achievement in tasks that gave meaning to the individual, ...hygiene factors do not relate to the task, so they are powerless to give such meaning" (Herzberg, 1962, p. 78). "Growth is dependent on some achievements, but achievement requires a task" (Herzberg, 1962, p. 78). When growth is accomplished, it is due to the culmination of prior accomplishments or tasks. "Task factors provide additional experience and information to be drawn upon that can be beneficial in reaching one's point of self-actualization" (Herzberg, 1962, p. 78). Motivation is an important component in providing job satisfaction because "there may be individuals who because of motivation and the things that have happened to them have learned to read positively the factors associated with the contexts of their jobs" (Herzberg, 1962, p. 80).

Another dynamic of motivation is self-concept of ability, which is the internal drive seeking to feel a sense of accomplishment. One may set goals; and by completing the goals, a sense of accomplishment is achieved. Thereby the process and or the steps that lead to achievement function as a motivator. The belief of an individual that a task or tasks can be accomplished propels one forward until the success is obtained (Davis & Wilson, 2000).

The equity theory of motivation conveys that individuals strive to maintain a balance between his or her output such as one's efforts, and input, what is to be received in response to one's output. When individuals, namely employees, perceive that there is an inequality between his or her output and an organization's input, the employee works to equalize the inequity, whether it may be an increase or decrease of output (Dessler, 1999). The observations from research studies support the equity theory, stating that the participants actively worked to balance their perceived inequity from their output and an organization's input (Dessler, 1999).

The expectancy theory of motivation implies that motivation rests on an individual's self-efficacy. Vroom generated a theory with three constructs of valence, instrumentality, and expectancy (Dessler, 1999). Valence represents that the value of goal achievement to an individual. Instrumentality represents one's perception of the importance of his or her role in the attainment of a goal. Lastly, is expectancy. Expectancy is what the individual perceives will occur from his or her output.

Locke's (1968) goal setting theory of motivation contends that specific, challenging goals, if accepted, will produce higher performance than the implementation of simplistic goals (Sagie & Koslowsky, 2000). Researchers have found better results from employees who participate in goal setting than from employees who do not participate in goal setting. Goal clarity is a function of goal setting and has been associated with positive school performance (Kelley, Odden, Milanowski, & Heneman; 2000).

Satisfaction is consistently present throughout the literature related to motivation and motivational theory. The ability to become satisfied with a task is attributed to one being motivated. Throughout each theory of motivation, a nexus is apparent between satisfaction and motivation, generated from one successfully reaching a motivational threshold, and thereafter progresses to the realm of satisfaction (Herzberg, 1959).

Job Involvement

As motivation functions as a subcomponent of job satisfaction, job involvement does as well. Each component affects satisfaction individually; however together the affect is intensified. Motivation energizes an sustains job involvement. Job involvement helps employees work towards goals (Ford, 1999). In addition, research by Igbaria, Parasuraman, & Badawy, (1994) found that employees who are highly involved also display high commitment to the organization. Job involvement is a key component necessary to the success of an organization because employees are enhanced by "power sharing, information sharing, knowledge training, and reward systems relevant to organization performance" (Pun, Chin, & Gill, 2001, p. 98).

At the beginning, job involvement initiatives were focused on improving the negative aspects of an employment relationship such as turnover, absenteeism, recruitment, and retention. However, current efforts have refocused the purpose of employee involvement to have a beneficial affect on the overall organization in terms of enhancing an organization's performance and effectiveness (Shapiro, 2000).

There are many advantages to implementing job involvement within an organization. Creating an environment that nurtures and supports the job involvement of employees is good for the organization because job involvement allows employees to be active contributors in multiple facets of their job, which facilitates an organization's growth (Pun, Chin, & Gill, 2001). High job involvement is also important because in today's society, employees need to be as flexible as possible in light of downsizing and lay offs (Axtell & Parker, 2003). Studies have shown that employee involvement is associated to employee well being (Riipinen, 1997).

Private industries have been exploring employee involvement efforts to improve performance. These efforts can be utilized in the field of education. There has been a significant rise in the number of companies implementing various forms of employee involvement (Lawler, Mohrman, & Benson; 2001). Improvements in the areas of productivity, quality, and employee motivation are general reasons companies report for implementing employee involvement programs (Lawler, Mohrman, & Ledford, 1995). Lawler, Mohrman, and Ledford (1995) report true involvement strategies elicit the participation of employees at the lower levels of the organization. For employees to be a valuable addition to the development and growth of an organization there must be a distribution of power, information, knowledge and rewards. Job involvement affects an employee's perception of his or her role and ability to perform in an organization (Dessler, 1999). Increased employee involvement leads to improved decision-making and successful initiative implementation (Mohrman, 1994). By allowing employee involvement in the planning process, before implementation, employees can help structure plans in a manner, which they believe will be successful (self-efficacy) and attractive to them (Lawler, 1986). Now that other industries have endured the trials and research of the implementation of increased job involvement, it is time for schools and school district to tailor job involvement to meet the needs of the employees in field of education.

The literature suggests that a large organization, such as a school or a school district would be an ideal candidate to implement employee involvement efforts because employees of large organizations often experience difficulties with motivation, communication, and coordination (Lawler, Mohrman, & Ledford, 1995; Lawler, Mohrman, & Benson, 2001). Job involvement personalizes activities for employees. Teachers' involvement in the decision-making process is critical to the restructuring and improving schools. Job involvement solicits the opinions and suggestions of employees. Employees feel valued and put their best effort forward. "Involvement enables employees to act at work within their authority, respond to solve problems, and to suggest feasible alternatives" (Pun, Chin, & Gill, 2001, p. 97). When decisions are made by teachers they may feel a greater sense of ownership with their decisions and may be more willing to provide a greater effort to ensure that their decisions are successfully executed. In contrast, when plans are implemented without the consent of teachers, there may be less consensus, effort, and enthusiasm towards the goals (Johnson & Landman, 2000). The results from research suggest that it is detrimental to the success of an organization to involve employees without providing them with enough information to make informed plans (Lawler, 1986). Information allows employees to learn more about the organization and the organization's future direction (Lawler, Mohrman, & Ledford; 1995). Researchers have found that advancements in the knowledge of employees results in improvements to the organization (Lawler, Mohrman, & Benson; 2001). Lawler, Mohrman, and Benson report that there is a significant relationship between employee involvement and their acquisition of knowledge. For employee involvement to be truly successful, employees must receive additional information about the organization and training (Lawler, Mohrman, & Benson; 2001). Moreover, without information about an organization's strengths and weaknesses the plans and efforts of employees may be futile (Lawler, Mohrman, & Ledford; 1995). Providing teachers with information about their school and its direction may generate promising results. Therefore, to enhance job satisfaction, job involvement should be implemented.

A significant motivational factor influencing the successful attainment of goals depends on the self-efficacy of the teacher (Kelley, Odden, Milanowski, & Heneman; 2000). Employee involvement should encourage employees to enhance their abilities to gain knowledge, develop skills, accept responsibility, and improve the overall performance of the organization (Lawler, Mohrman, & Benson; 2001). It is essential to the academic achievement and educational progress of students to increase teachers' job involvement, and thereby advance their self-efficacy. Social cognitive theory suggests that motivation is influenced by self-efficacy. "Perceived self-efficacy is defined as people's beliefs about their capabilities to produce designated levels of performance that exercise influence over events that affect their lives" (Bandura, p. 71, 1994). Therefore the more one believes he or she is capable of doing a task, the more one will be motivated to do the task. Bandura has found that individuals who have low self-efficacy tend to avoid completing tasks that require skills that individuals perceive they do not have. In addition, Bandura states that high efficacy individuals are capable of applying high efforts in the face of challenges. In regards to teachers, this may mean a greater degree of success with the education of students (Wilson & Coolican, 1996). Motivating teachers to apply more effort improves the possibility for success from the belief that the goal is attainable. Moreover, the teacher-student relationship is greatly influenced by the self-efficacy of the teacher (Enderlin-Lampe, 2002). Researchers found that teachers' self-efficacy is a significant predictor of the success of students. Therefore, it is imperative to empower and support the development of teachers (Mulford & Silins, 2002).

Researchers have found that there is a negative relationship between job involvement and employee turnover, or as employee involvement decreases, employee turnover increases. Therefore, as a means of reducing levels of attrition efforts to increase employee involvement may be implemented (Sjöberg & Sverke, 2000). In education, professional learning communities utilize increased job involvement. Professional learning communities seem to have beneficial effects on not only the teachers, but the students as well (Harris, 2002). By increasing the job involvement of teachers to encompass collaborative relationships and the decision-making process, significant improvements may be achieved in educating students (Davis & Wilson, 2000).

With every situation there are pros and cons. With the implementation of employee involvement endeavors the pros appear to significantly outweigh the cons. Positive results have been reported from companies that have employee involvement programs (Lawler, Mohrman, & Ledford; 1995).

Employee involvement in the decision-making process may bring several beneficial factors such as reduced alienation and increased feelings of belongingness (Sagie & Koslowsky, 2000). In addition, as involvement increases job satisfaction increases (Sagie & Koslowsky, 2000). Moreover, results from studies suggest that companies that utilize employee involvement efforts are more productive and the employees are more satisfied (Mohrman, 1994). High involvement also provides significant beneficial factors to not only the organization, but the employee as well. Studies have found that employees who display high job involvement exhibit high self esteem as a result of their participation (Janssen, 2003). Job involvement has many beneficial effects such as increased employee satisfaction, quality performance, enhanced productivity, higher motivation, improved decision-making, growth, and less resistance to change (Lawler, 1986; Pun, Chin, & Gill, 2001).

Involvement – Empowerment

Researchers have found that empowerment is one of the strategies that may be used to increase job involvement, other strategies may include job enrichment, job enlargement, autonomous work groups, and empowerment (Pun, Chin, & Gill; 2001). Empowerment is an essential part of uniting employees and deriving the most from employees. Empowerment authorizes employees to initiate and implement their plans (Talbert, 2003).

The force and power of job involvement can be attributed empowerment. Empowerment allows employees more control and input on their work related tasks, thereby giving them a reason to want to be successful and adding to the satisfaction that they may experience. Moreover, the literature suggests that empowerment also elicits feelings of satisfaction by providing teachers the authority to produce successful endeavors. "Empowerment is a process of heightening the motivation of employees to accomplish job related tasks" (Conger & Kanungo, 1988; Wilson & Coolican, 1996, p. 99). Researchers have found that employees will have increased motivation to accomplish a goal, if it is directly related to their personal interest (McClelland, 1975; Wilson & Coolican; 1996).

Tyack (1993) believes that public school teachers are not given the respect and the power that is required for them to make significant changes in education due to the strongholds that policy makers have infringed on their scope of authority (Tyack, 1997). Throughout the school systems there are factors that limit teacher empowerment. An ethnographic research report states that some of the factors that prohibit teacher empowerment are (a) fear of participation in school based decision-making, (b) lack of representation of teacher participants in decision-making committees, (c) limited activism by teachers, and (d) perceived disconnectedness from the process of policy implementation (Talbert, 2003).

Throughout the nation, there is an urge for an increase in teacher participation in the schools' decision-making process to improve reform initiatives. Research studies suggest that the implementation of empowerment with employees has positive benefits on an organization. One of the advantages of employee empowerment is increased workforce commitment. Increased commitment leads to good work environment, high quality work life, and good employee relations (Paul, Niehoff, & Turnely; 2000). Teachers have first hand experience of the needs and abilities of students. Given the opportunity to participate in school endeavors, teachers may significantly enhance the plans for schools direction and student instruction (Enderlin-Lampe, 2002).

Moreover, many academics and reformers argue that teachers are not interested in job involvement or an increase in responsibility – haven't you heard the teachers across America consistently state they are overworked and underpaid? Empowerment is not about increasing the responsibility of teachers. Empowerment is about giving teachers the authority to make positive changes and innovations in the field of education (Spillane, 1999).

> Teachers who are empowered have actively participated in the development of personal strengths and ideas; defined rationales and goals of their own professional development in content and pedagogical knowledge; embraced provisions of continuous year long support aimed at breaking down isolation and building cooperation, collation, and collegiality between themselves, their colleagues, their students and the education community at large; and engaged in efforts to increase their knowledge base, thorough such means as special in-service networking, peer coaching, and mentoring. (Runyan, 1991, p. 9)

Job involvement is not only important to the success of teachers, it is also important to the success of the students. Mulford and Silins (2003) found that schools are more likely to experience success if the teachers are empowered and involved in school related functions. In addition, success may be found with increasing teacher participation in the design phase of reform efforts (Spillane, Henderson, & Diamond; 2004).

A study found that 66% of Fortune 100 Companies utilize employee involvement efforts to improve operations in their organizations. Organizations are eager to implement employee empowerment efforts because researchers have found advantages associated with the empowerment of employees such as higher quality output, less absenteeism, lower turnover, improved decision-making, and enhanced problem solving, which improves the overall operations of an organization (Paul, et al., 2000). Job involvement may be one of the missing elements to promote teachers' accomplishments in the classroom and the school (Burr & Cordery, 2001).

Many researchers state in regards to learning, information must be meaningful. Individuals must evaluate the advantages and the disadvantages that are associated with each task. It is vital for employers to keep employees interested in work related tasks. Employers are more likely to reap benefits from interested employees. Employees may withdraw and become complacent in their approach towards work related responsibilities when they are not significantly involved. However, with increased responsibility and input, which is defined by empowerment, a meaningful difference may be noticed with the performance and satisfaction of employees (Herzberg, 1959).

Internal promotions have been found to have a positive affect on the job satisfaction of employees. Although not exactly the same, there are comparable characteristics between an increase in job involvement and promotions. Therefore, some of the same positive benefits may be displayed when the job involvement of employees is increased (Johnston, Griffeth, Burton, & Carson; 1999).

Studies suggest that employees like to have a voice in work related functions. The empowerment of employees may manifest into a force, which is capable of speaking to express the motivations that are within each individual. When motivations are expressed and realized, satisfaction concerning one's job is more likely to be achieved (Herzberg, 1962). Davis and Wilson (2000) state that it is a common belief in the field of education that job satisfaction is positively correlated with the amount of teacher participation in decision-making activities.

Job satisfaction is clearly related to levels of intrinsic empowerment. Job satisfaction refers to individuals' affective relations to their work role and is a function of the perceived relationship between what one wants from one's job and what one perceives it is offering (Lawler, 1973; Locke, 1969; Davis & Wilson, 2000, p. 350).

Many researchers have found that the empowerment of employees increases employee satisfaction. When employees are empowered, they feel more ownership and commitment in the tasks associated with their employment. Motivation is given a forceful direction courtesy of empowerment. When employees are empowered, new enthusiasm arises that was not present before. Employees are capable of having an increased impact, interest, or vigor in the manner which they approach their job; however, all of these actions are attributable to the internal drives of an individual (Herzberg, 1959).

Given the information that has been presented on job involvement, it is clear that job satisfaction is an important element. Job involvement functions to allow employees to have increased responsibility and input with their organization, which may increase their self-efficacy, and thereby produce feelings of satisfaction.

Compensation

In the 1800's there was great disparity in the compensation of teachers. The disparity existed among the school levels, races, and genders. There have been significant advancements in the equalization of the compensation schedule of teachers. The equalization can be attributed to the single salary schedule, which awards compensation based upon years of experience and the highest level of education attained. Many research studies have been employed to determine if years of experience and level of education impact the academic achievement of students, and the results of the studies suggest that neither variable significantly impacts the academic achievement of students. Many individuals in the field of education feel that it is more justifiable to compensate teachers based upon their ability to educate students rather than their years of experience and level of academic achievement (Odden, 1995).

Reward systems function to supplement the efforts of employee involvement. The literature on employee involvement strongly suggests utilizing reward systems along with employee involvement endeavors (Lawler, Mohrman, & Benson; 2001). Rewards may facilitate employees' development of self-worth and achievement, as a result of their involvement in work related activities (Lawler, 1986). Lawler, Mohrman, and Benson (2001) report that performance can be affected by rewards. Monetary and non-monetary incentives can be useful in augmenting employee involvement programs (Lawler, Mohrman, & Ledford; 1995). Seventy-five percent of respondents state that they have had positive results from the implementation of non-monetary recognition efforts (Lawler, Mohrman, & Ledford; 1995). Theorists contend that rewards and sanctions help focus teachers on the primary instructional goals; and thereafter, teachers apply clarified efforts to reach goals (Lashway, 2001). Moreover, teachers reported that sanctions function as motivators for them to actively work towards increasing students' achievement (Kelley, Odden, Milanowski, & Heneman; 2000). Studies suggest that there is also an increase in employees' satisfaction when additional motivators are used to influence their performance (Sagie & Koslowsky, 2000).

There has been extensive research and implementation of various compensation packages beyond the single salary schedule without distinguishable gains to student achievement. Some of the big initiatives of compensation were merit pay, career ladder, and various forms of state created incentive packages. Many of the incentives and compensation plans were discontinued due to the lack of success found from their implementation. Merit pay and career ladder pay had limited success because of the rivalry that they created among teachers. The rivalry grew from teachers competing for a limited amount of funds (Cornett & Gaines, 2002; Kelley & Odden, 1995).

Pay for performance, skill or competency-based pay, pay-at-risk, compensation for certification, and the group-based performance awards are forms of compensation plans that have received notoriety for their ability to justify teachers' compensation (Goorian, 2000; Kelley & Odden, 1995). One of the most promising compensation schemes is the group-based performance award. Group-based performance awards provide all members of the school additional compensation when the desired level of students' academic achievement is achieved. Group-based performance awards are popular because they promote team building and collaborative efforts, unlike other forms of individual-based performance awards (Brown, 2002).

Compensation is not always the problem or the answer. A researcher points out that, although private school teachers often earn less than public school teachers they often experience greater satisfaction courtesy of high staff morale, being valued, and being supported (Hess, 2004). Teacher labor statistics often report high rates of teacher attrition, such as 12 to 20%, for first year teachers. Incentive programs should start to focus on the professional growth and development of the nearly 90% of teachers that remain in the field of teaching year after year (Cornett & Gaines, 2002).

Many industries have decentralized and restructured their management leadership, to form shared leadership. Shared leadership alters and augments the responsibility of employees (Odden, 1995). If the restructuring of employees' jobs and responsibilities is to be successful, employees must be compensated for their efforts. Properly utilized, compensation plans may have a very positive effect on the academic achievement of students. A significant increase in students' academic achievement was observed in a study where a detailed compensation plan was implemented to compensate teachers for students' academic achievement. The results demonstrated over a 40% increase in student achievement over four years (Lafee, 2003).

Incentives and bonuses allow employees to reap the rewards from their efforts with their students and improvements to their knowledge and skills. These rewards function as motivators for many employees (Lawler, Mohrman, & Ledford; 1995). Teachers have expressed a strong affinity for pay incentives in regards to improvements in their knowledge and skills (Kelley, Odden, Milanowski, & Heneman; 2000). Many researchers promote that bonuses and incentives are not good because they are external motivators; however, the results from a recent study imply that bonuses are a valuable addition to an accountability system (Lashway, 2001).

Compensation has frequently been reported as a problem of teachers. In some areas of the country, school districts are implementing alternative compensation plans that provide additional compensation to teachers that take steps to improve their knowledge and skills, which may enhance students achievement (Odden & Kelley, 2000). The use of incentives may capture the motivation of additional teachers, which previous research suggests may have a positive affect on students' academic achievement

(Lashway, 2001). Researchers have found that teachers are very motivated to improve students' academic achievement when provided with monetary motivators based on students' exhibited improvements (Hopkin, 1997). Odden and Kelley (2000) report that teachers agreed that improvements in students' performance based on their instructional efforts warranted bonuses. Offering monetary motivators as an incentive for exemplary teaching strategies may reduce some of teachers' feelings of dissatisfaction with their compensation and improve their instructional performance (Odden & Kelley, 2000). Evidence from research studies suggest that alternative forms of compensation may have positive affects on teachers' motivation (Odden & Kelley, 2000). Results from a research study found that 75% of teachers confirmed that they were motivated by additional compensation for improvements to their knowledge and skills (Odden & Kelley, 2000). However, in order to motivate teachers with bonuses and incentives the amount of the bonus must be carefully evaluated to determine if teachers will find the bonus of significant value (Odden & Kelley, 2000). Researchers have found that bonuses must be at least 5 to 8% of a teacher's salary to affect his or her motivation (Odden & Kelley, 2000). Rewards provide teachers with the opportunity to attain a successful outcome, which research has shown to produce satisfaction. From the literature it is clear that rewards linked to job involvement may produce feelings of satisfaction in some teachers.

Summary

Despite the elaborate reform efforts and initiatives that have been implemented across America, a significant area of education has been neglected, the job satisfaction of teachers. Job satisfaction is an important component in the relationship between an employer and an employee. Teachers experience a variety of issues that may inhibit them from experiencing satisfaction. Teachers have significant roles, if not the most significant roles in the lives of students. Gaining an enhanced understanding of the extent that teachers' traits may be able to predict their job satisfaction could potentially be the key to improving reform efforts and initiatives. Professional development is a wonderful tool available to assist in the professional growth of teachers. Professional development, in the form of professional learning communities can be an exciting way to increase the job involvement and professional growth of teachers, and thereby facilitate the academic achievement of students. Professional learning communities allow teachers to create and exchange meaningful strategies to enhance the academic achievement of students. In addition, compensation is another important component in providing significant improvement to teachers' job satisfaction. Studies have shown positive gains in the academic achievement of students whose teachers were compensated above the base salary for improved student achievement (Hopkins, 1997). This chapter reviewed the literature related to the negative outcome of teaching, professional development, professional learning communities, job satisfaction, motivation, motivational theory, job involvement, and compensation. The next chapter discusses the methodology used in this research study.

CHAPTER THREE

Method

Introduction

The previous chapter reviewed the literature related to the negative outcomes of teaching, professional development, professional learning communities, job satisfaction, motivation, motivational theory, job involvement, and compensation. The purpose of this study was to describe the extent to which teachers' traits (as perceived job involvement, perceived motivation, level of instruction, stipend recipient, and years of teaching experience) predict the job satisfaction of teachers. The literature suggests that in the business arena the motivation employees possess to complete work related tasks significantly influences the satisfaction they experience (Herzberg, 1959). This study attempted to examine similar factors, except among teachers in the field of education. The methodology used to conduct this study is described in this chapter. This chapter includes the following information: (a) the research design, (b) the participants, (c) the research setting (d) the instrument design, (e) the data collection procedures, (f) the data analysis procedures, and (g) the limitations of the study.

Research Design

Many research designs were analyzed and reviewed to determine the best approach to collect the data from the participants. Ultimately, a survey research design was chosen to collect data to describe the traits of teachers. Survey methods were utilized because of the many advantages they provide, i.e., the ability to generalize to an entire population, cost effectiveness, and time efficiency. A survey also allows a participant to generate a self-report, which may be very useful in gathering the data (Gall, Borg, & Gall, 1996; Penner, 1999). Fowler (1993) has reported, "…there are numerous facts about the behavior and situations of the people that can be obtained only by asking a sample of people about themselves" (p. 2). Multiple linear regression and correlation analyses were utilized to explain the relationship between the variables. The criterion variable was job satisfaction and the predictor variables were perceived job involvement, perceived motivation, level of instruction, stipend recipient, and years of teaching experience. These variables were quantified through the use of measures, which provided scores based on the perceptions and actualities of teachers.

Participants

There were 52 participants from two elementary schools, one middle school, and one high school in the Houston Independent School District (HISD). HISD is the largest district in Texas and the seventh largest district in the United States. The district was chosen because of its diversity and large number of employees. HISD has more than 300 campuses and approximately 13,000 teachers. The participants of this study taught in grade levels from early childhood to the 12th grade. The participants were of various racial backgrounds, i.e., African American, Asian, Hispanic, and White. The participants were non-paid volunteers whose ages ranged from 21-70 years. The participants had various years of teaching experience. The participants were both male and female.

Research Setting

The schools, which participated in the study, Askew Elementary, Walnut Bend Elementary, Paul Revere Middle, and Westside High, are located in the west administrative district in HISD. HISD currently has 13 administrative districts; however, HISD is in the process of reducing the administrative districts from 13 to 3. The west district is frequently characterized as one of the better sub-districts within HISD because of high student performance on standardized tests. This section includes additional information about each of the schools from past schools years from the School Profile Reports provided by HISD and the Academic Excellence Indicator System (AEIS) provided by the Texas Education Agency (TEA) (HISD, 2005; TEA, 2005). The Academic Excellence Indicator System is a system designed to evaluate the performance of schools and school districts in the state of Texas based on a multitude of criteria, a few being student demographics, student performance, compliance, and data integrity. There are four ratings available for districts and schools. For districts, the ratings are exemplary, recognized, academically acceptable, and academically unacceptable. For schools, the ratings are Exemplary, Recognized, Acceptable, and Low Performing. During the 2003-2004 school, as a district HISD received the rating of "Academically Acceptable" from TEA. The table below presents the previous ratings of HISD by TEA.

Table 1

Accountability Rating for HISD from TEA

	98-99	99-00	00-01	01-02	02-03
Performance	Academically Acceptable	Academically Acceptable	Academically Acceptable	Academically Acceptable	*N/A

* Ratings not assigned 2002-2003 School Year

The first school addressed is Askew Elementary. Askew Elementary is located at 11200 Woodlodge in Houston, TX. The school had over 800 students in grades PK-4. The student body had diverse ethnicities, which included 28% African American, 10% Asian, 34% Hispanic, less than 1% Native American, and 28% White (HISD, 2005).

During the 2002-2003 school year the student attendance rate was approximately 96%. The student mobility rate was 27%. The school did not provide in-school-suspension; however, the school reported 31 out-of-school suspensions for various behavioral infractions (HISD, 2005; TEA, 2005).

Askew Elementary offered a variety of programs to serve the special needs of the students, which included advanced academics, special education, and multilingual education. Advanced academics was comprised of the Neighborhood Gifted & Talented (G/T) Program and the Vanguard Program. Thirty-one percent of the students were identified as G/T. The special education program provided a number of services including behavior and resource services, and speech therapy. The special education program served 6% of the students. Multilingual education provided services to 22% of the students who were identified as LEP (Limited English Proficiency) students. Multilingual education included the Bilingual program and the ESL (English as a Second Language) program. The Bilingual program provided instruction in Spanish and English to LEP students. The ESL program utilizes instructional strategies to improve the academic achievement of LEP students who may speak Spanish or languages other than English. As of the 2003-2004 school year, Askew Elementary became a 100% Title 1 School. Title 1 provides schools with additional funds to educate disadvantaged students (U.S. Department of Education, 2005). Fifty-two percent of the students were labeled economically disadvantaged and 36% of the students were labeled at-risk of dropping out of school.

In 2004, Askew Elementary received a "Recognized" school accountability rating from the Texas Education Agency. Together, the students of Askew Elementary scored above the state and district average for their academic performance in Reading / English Language Arts, Mathematics, Writing, and all tests combined. Askew Elementary also was commended for the students' performance in the area of Reading / English Language Arts (HISD, 2005; TEA, 2005). The table below presents the previous ratings of Askew Elementary by TEA.

Table 2

Accountability Rating for Askew Elementary from TEA

	98-99	99-00	00-01	01-02	02-03
Performance	Acceptable	Recognized	Acceptable	Recognized	*N/A

* Ratings not assigned 2002-2003 School Year

Askew Elementary had a staff of 67. There were 52 teachers, which included 25% African American, 4% Asian, 11% Hispanic, and 60% White. Twelve percent of the teachers were male and 88% of the teachers were female. The average teacher at Askew Elementary had 12 years of teaching experience. Nineteen percent of the teachers possessed a Master's degree. In addition to the teachers, there were three paraprofessionals, two campus administrators, 10 educational aides, and other members (HISD, 2005; TEA, 2005).

The next school addressed is Walnut Bend Elementary. Walnut Bend Elementary is located at 10620 Briar Forest in Houston, TX. The school had over 700 students in grades EC-5. The student body had diverse ethnicities, which included 26% African American, 4% Asian, 46% Hispanic, and 24% White (HISD, 2005; TEA, 2005).

During the 2002-2003 school year the student attendance rate was approximately 96%. The student mobility rate was 23%. The school did not provide in-school suspension; however the school reported 14 out-of-school suspensions for various behavioral infractions (HISD, 2005; TEA, 2005).

Walnut Bend offered a variety of programs to serve the special needs of the students, which included advanced academics, special education, and multilingual education. Advanced academics was comprised of the Neighborhood Gifted & Talented (G/T) Program. Eleven percent of the students were identified as G/T. The special education program provided a number of services including generic self-contained class, resource services, and speech therapy. The special education program served 10% of the students. Multilingual education provided services to 37% of the students who were identified as LEP students. Multilingual education included the Bilingual program and the ESL program. As of the 2003-2004 school year, Walnut Bend Elementary became a 100% Title 1 School. Sixty-four percent of the students were labeled economically disadvantaged and 36% of the students were labeled at-risk of dropping out of school. In 2004, Walnut Bend Elementary received an "Academically Acceptable" school accountability rating from the Texas Education Agency (HISD, 2005; TEA, 2005). The table below presents the previous ratings of Walnut Bend Elementary by TEA.

Table 3

Accountability Rating for Walnut Bend Elementary from TEA

	98-99	99-00	00-01	01-02	02-03
Performance	Acceptable	Acceptable	Acceptable	Acceptable	*N/A

* Ratings not assigned 2002-2003 School Year

Walnut Bend Elementary had a staff of 60. There were 50 teachers, which included 13% African American, 2% Asian, 11% Hispanic, and 24% White. Eight percent of the teachers were male and 92% of the teachers were female. The average teacher at Walnut Bend Elementary had 14 years of teaching experience. Twenty-five percent of the teachers possessed a Master's degree and two percent possessed a doctorate degree. In addition to the teachers, there were three paraprofessionals, 1 campus administrators, and six educational aides (HISD, 2005; TEA, 2005).

The next school addressed is Paul Revere Middle. Paul Revere Middle is located at 10502 Briar Forest in Houston, TX. The school had over 1200 students in grades 6-8. The student body had diverse ethnicities, which included 34% African American, 8% Asian, 47% Hispanic, and 11% White (HISD, 2005; TEA, 2005).

During the 2002-2003 school year the student attendance rate was approximately 95%. The student mobility rate was 27%. The school reported 1,095 in-school suspensions, 990 out-of-school suspensions, 3 expulsions, 58 alternative placements, thereby creating a total of 2146 various behavioral remediation efforts (HISD, 2005; TEA, 2005).

The school offered a variety of programs to serve the special needs of the students, which included advanced academics, a magnet program, special education, multilingual education, and career and technology education. Advanced academics was comprised of the Pre-AP (Advanced Placement) Program, also known as Honors classes. Thirty-four percent of the students participated in Honors classes. Nine percent of the students were identified as G/T. The specializations of the Magnet program were math and science. The special education program provided a number of services such as behavior services, inclusion, life skills, resource services, and speech therapy. The special education program served 11% of the students. Multilingual education provided services to 16% of the students who were identified as LEP students. Multilingual education provided the ESL program. Career and Technology education included classes devoted to career investigation, introductory to horticulture, and technology education. Fourteen percent of the students participated in Career and Technology education. As of the 2003-2004 Paul Revere Middle became a 100% Title 1 School. Seventy-four percent of the students were labeled economically disadvantaged and 48% of the students were labeled at-risk of dropping out of school. In 2004, Paul Revere Middle received an "Academically Acceptable" school accountability rating from the Texas Education Agency (HISD, 2005; TEA, 2005). The table below presents the previous ratings of Paul Revere Middle by TEA.

Table 4

Accountability Rating for Paul Revere Middle from TEA

	98-99	99-00	00-01	01-02	02-03
Performance	Recognized	Recognized	Acceptable	Recognized	*N/A

* Ratings not assigned 2002-2003 School Year

Paul Revere Middle had a staff of 90. There were 76 teachers, which included 28% African American, 3% Asian, 9% Hispanic, and 36% White. Thirty-two percent of the teachers were male and 68% of the teachers were female. The average teacher at Paul Revere Middle had 13 years of teaching experience. Thirty-four percent of the teachers possessed a Master's degree and one percent possessed a doctorate degree. In addition to the teachers, there were six paraprofessionals, five campus administrators, and three educational aides (HISD, 2005; TEA, 2005).

The last school addressed is Westside High. Westside High school opened in 2000. Westside High is located at 14201 Briar Forest in Houston, TX. The school had over 2800 students in grades 9-12. The student body had diverse ethnicities, which included 26% African American, 9% Asian, 28% Hispanic, and 36% White.

During the 2002-2003 school year the student attendance rate was approximately 94%. The student mobility rate was 17%. There were 378 students in the graduating class. The student dropout rate was reported as 2.1% The school reported 460 in-school suspensions, 272 out-of-school suspensions, and 51 alternative placements, thereby creating a total of 783 various behavioral remediation efforts (HISD, 2005; TEA, 2005).

The school offered a variety of programs to serve the special needs of the students, which included advanced academics, a magnet program, special education, multilingual education, and career and technology education. Advanced academics was comprised of the Pre-AP (Advanced Placement) and AP Program, also known as Honors classes. Forty-nine percent of the students participated in Honors classes. Sixteen percent of the students were identified as G/T. The specialization of the Magnet program was Integrated Technology. Special education provided a number of services including behavior services, content mastery, employment specialist, inclusion, life skills, resource services, speech therapy, and vocational adjustment class (VAC). The special education program served 11% of the students. Multilingual education provided services to 16% of the students who were identified as LEP students. Multilingual education included the ESL program. Career and Technology education included classes devoted to business / office education, T & I Computer Maintenance, T & I Culinary Arts, and Technology Education. Twenty-eight percent of the students were labeled economically disadvantaged and 51% of the students were labeled at-risk of dropping out of school. In 2004, Westside High received an "Academically Acceptable" school accountability rating from the Texas Education Agency (HISD, 2005; TEA, 2005).

Table 5

Accountability Rating for Westside High School from TEA

	00-01	01-02	02-03
Performance	Acceptable	Low-Performing	*N/A

* Ratings not assigned 2002-2003 School Year

Westside High had a staff of 162. There were 142 teachers, which included 15% African American, 5% Asian, 6% Hispanic, and 75% White. Forty-six percent of the teachers were male and 54% of the teachers were female. The average teacher at Westside High had 11 years of teaching experience. Thirty percent of the teachers possessed a Master's degree and three percent possessed a doctorate degree. In addition to the teachers, there were four paraprofessionals, five campus administrators, five educational aides, and additional members (HISD, 2005; TEA, 2005).

Instruments

The Teacher Involvement and Participation Scale (TIPS 2) was utilized to measure the job involvement of teachers. The TIPS 2 was created by Dr. J. J. Russell in his dissertation study in 1992 at Fordham University. The TIPS 2 is a 22-item scale that measures teachers' involvement and participation in their educational organization (Russell, 1992).

The TIPS 2 was chosen because of its ability to measure the extent teachers currently participate in the planning of curriculum, policies, and decision-making at their school. It is important to the success of schools that teachers participate and are involved in planning and implementing school related endeavors (Enderline-Lampe, 2002).

The TIPS 2 scale was given to 109 teachers at five different schools. Two of the schools were reported to have high levels of shared decision-making, two schools were reported to have low levels of shared decision-making, and the fifth and final school was reported to have a moderate level of shared decision-making (Russell, 1992).

Multiple reliability analyses were done on the measure to ensure the results were reliable. The Cronbach alpha, Spearman-Brown, and Guttman split-half techniques were utilized on the data gathered from the 109 teachers from the five different schools to assess the reliability of the measure. The alpha coefficient for the TIPS 2 was assessed to be .96 (Russell, 1992).

The review of the literature concerning teacher involvement and participation guided the creation of the TIPS 2. Eight areas were chosen to be a part of the 22-item measure. Face validity was established using a panel of experts to determine a high degree of correlation with each of the eight areas. Only statements that had at least 80% agreement among all panel members were included in the measure (Russell, 1992).

The next measure utilized during the study was the Self-Motivation Index. The Self-Motivation Index was created by Dishman and Gettman (1980) and was used to measure the motivation of teachers. The Self-Motivation Index has also been used in the dissertation study by Merkle (1997) at the University of Houston and many other studies to determine the motivation of individuals in regards to work. The Self-Motivation Inventory was chosen because of its ability to measure the propensity one has to work related tasks. From the results generated by the data, it may be determined that there is a correlation between motivation and the other variables.

The Self-Motivation Index is a 60-item questionnaire with a 5-point Likert response scale, which represented to what degree each statement was characteristic or uncharacteristic of one's personality. The original 60-item questionnaire was given to over 400 males and females enrolled in an undergraduate psychology course "(mean age + standard deviation 19.1 + 1.46 years, range 17-27)" (Merkle, 1997, p. 31). The items from the questionnaire were correlated with self-reported data and the total scores were calculated. The items that did not adequately measure the variable were removed. Thereafter, the remaining 48-items were further tested by an alpha factor analysis with a varimax rotation and a subsequent deletion of surplus items followed. This left a total of 40 questions (Merkle, 1997). The scores have a possible range of 40-200. Greater scores signify increased motivation. Test-retest reliability was established by re-administering the survey to the sample group of students one month later, which yielded a correlation coefficient of .92.

The questionnaire was validated by face validity with the samples of participants. The researchers verified that the index measures what it purports to measure by analyzing the results from the survey participants. Thereby affirming that the participants interpreted the items in the way the items were meant to be interpreted (Dishman & Gettman, 1997).

The Job Satisfaction Index authored by Brayfield and Rothe (1951) was utilized to determine the perceived job satisfaction of teachers. The Job Satisfaction Index has been used numerous times since its creation in 1951 to measure the job satisfaction of employees. The Job Satisfaction Index was selected because of its continuous use throughout the years and its ability to measure the extent participants are satisfied with their jobs.

Reliability was established through test-retest administration of the index to the study participants. The reliability was reported to be .87. According to the authors of the index, each of the items has face validity, and the index measures what it purports to measure. The index contains 18-items, which were created to give an overall index of job satisfaction rather than one that provides for specific item analysis.

Data Collection Procedures

Permission to gather data was obtained from the Human Subjects Committee at the University of Houston and the Research and Accountability Department of the Houston Independent School District. The researcher obtained individual consent from each of the participants. The schools selected to participate in the study were located within the same feeder pattern, which was located in the west sub district of the Houston

Independent School District, in west Houston. The following schools participated in the study: Askew Elementary, which has a total of 52 teachers, Walnut Bend Elementary, which has a total of 50 teachers, Paul Revere Middle, which has a total of 90 teachers, and Westside High School, which 89 teachers were given a survey; thereby creating a cumulative total of 281. The 281 questionnaires were placed in the teachers' boxes at each of the schools. The questionnaires were self-administered by each of the participants of the study. The participants read and followed the instructions that were given with the questionnaires. Thereafter, the teachers returned their questionnaires to a receptacle in the front office or the workroom of their school. Teachers' email addresses were retrieved from the Global Address Book, a feature in Outlook for HISD employees, and the teachers received a follow-up email requesting that they complete and return the survey that was placed in each teacher's box. The researcher returned to each of the schools to collect the surveys. A total of 52 surveys were collected from the schools that participated in the study, thereby creating a return rate of 18.5%.

Data Analysis Procedures

Descriptive statistics were utilized to determine the mean, median, mode, standard deviation, and frequency distribution for the demographics of the teachers and the measures. Multiple linear regression and correlation analyses were utilized to determine the extent of the relationship among the variables. The Pearson Product-Moment correlation coefficient (r) was used to express the degree of the relationship among the variables. In addition, multiple R, R squared, and adjusted R were used to describe the findings of the analyses. For the analyses, the 95% confidence level ($p < .05$) was used as the critical value for determining statistical significance. Educational significance was set at .28.

Limitations

This study was not executed under perfect conditions. The participants of this study worked in schools located in the west sub district of the Houston Independent School District, in west Houston. There were many factors that created limitations to this study. The factors include, but are not limited to the climate of the schools, the population of the teachers, and the population of the students, a lack of generalizability, low response rate, and the volunteer participants' self-reports to the self-administered surveys.

The participants of the survey may have served as a limitation for a number of reasons. An adequate sample of teachers was selected to participate in the study. Nineteen percent chose to participate in the study. Eighty-one percent did not to participate in the study. The responses of the 81% of participants may have been significantly different than the responses of those who chose participate. There are many factors that may have contributed to the lack of teachers' participation in the study including, but not limited to: substantial amounts of paperwork, extra duties, and the preparation of students for upcoming standardized tests. All of these duties contribute teachers' inability to accomplish additional unexpected tasks requested of them. In addition, the personal circumstances of the participants may have served as another limitation to the study. Each teacher may have had a multitude of factors affecting his or her ability to successfully carry out duties and extra tasks requested of him or her at work.

Volunteer participants were another source of limitation to this study. The volunteer effect states that volunteers differ from those who did not volunteer. Moreover volunteers may choose not participate due to the focus of a study. The volunteers were requested to complete self-administered surveys, in contrast to the surveys being administered by an interviewer. The participants may have misinterpreted items throughout the surveys. An interviewer could have clarified any ambiguous items. The participants responded to the closed-ended items of the survey. The closed-ended items could have served as a limitation because the participants' true responses were not available, and the next best responses were chosen. The participants gave self-reports. The reports from the participants were only as accurate as the participants reported. Relying on the self-reports of the participants may have caused another limitation, having researchers observe the behavior of the participants may have reduced or eliminated this limitation.

Another source of limitation may have been the leadership of the school. School leadership may be described as the approach, behavior, and climate that campus administrators establish in a school. The approach, behavior, and climate significantly affect the members of the school including the teachers, staff, and the students. Therefore, the overall effect of the campus leadership may have functioned as a limitation to the study.

The students of the school may have served as a limitation. Students have a significant deal of interaction with teachers. Therefore, it is reasonable to expect that issues revolving around students may have diminished the participants' ability to respond to the survey. Thereby, the students of the schools that participated in this study may have served as a limitation.

CHAPTER FOUR

Results

This chapter presents the findings from the data analysis of the collected data as described in the previous chapter. The purpose of this study was to describe the extent to which the specified factors predicted the job satisfaction of teachers. The data analysis was completed by utilizing multiple regression statistical procedures. The criterion variable was job satisfaction and the predictor variables were measures of teachers' perceived involvement and participation, measures of teachers' perceived motivation, level of instruction, stipend recipient, and years of teaching experience. The sections of this chapter include (a) demographic data, (b) the research questions and their respective hypotheses, (c) additional findings, and (d) a summary.

Demographic Data

TABLE 6

Descriptive Statistics of Participants' Gender

	Frequency	Percent
Male	6	11.5
Female	46	88.5
Total	52	100.0

The participants of this study were a sample of teachers from the Houston Independent School District. There were 52 participants in the study. According to the self-reports of the participants there were 46 females and 6 males.

TABLE 7

Descriptive Statistics of Participants' Ethnicity

	Frequency	Percent
African American	12	23.1
Asian	4	7.7
Hispanic	5	9.6
White	31	59.6
Total	52	100.0

The ethnicity breakdown of the participants was 23.1% African American, 7.7% Asian, 9.6% Hispanic, and 59.6% White.

TABLE 8

Descriptive Statistics of Participants' Age

	Frequency	Percent
20-29	10	19.2
30-39	10	19.2
40-49	13	25.0
50-59	16	30.8
60-69	3	5.8
Total	52	100.0

The participants' ages were placed into ten-year ranges, represented by the following: (a) 19.2% were between the ages of 20-29 years, (b) 19.2% were between the ages of 30-39 years, (c) 25% were between the ages of 40-49 years, (d) 30.8% were between the ages of 50-59 years, and (e) 3% were between the ages of 60-69 years.

TABLE 9

Descriptive Statistics of Participants' Years of Teaching Experience

	Frequency	Percent
1-5	14	26.9
6-10	13	25.0
11-15	5	9.6
16-20	9	17.3
21-25	4	7.7
26+	7	13.5
Total	52	100.0

The participants of the study had various years of teaching experience that were represented by six intervals of five years. Twenty-six percent of the participants had 1-5 years of experience, 25% of the participants had 6-10 years of experience, 9.6% of the participants had 11-15 years of experience, 17.3% of the participants had 16-20 years of experience, 7.7% of the participants had 21-25 years of experience, and 13.5% of the participants had over 26 years of experience.

TABLE 10

Descriptive Statistics of Participants' Current Grade Level

	Frequency	Percent
EC-5	21	40.4
6-8	14	26.9
9-12	17	32.7
Total	52	100.0

The participants of the study taught in levels from early childhood (EC) to the twelfth grade, which were divided into three categories of EC-5th, 6th-8th, and 9th-12th. Forty percent of the teachers taught in the grade levels of EC-5th, 26.9% of the teachers taught in the grade levels of 6th -8th, and 32.7% of the teachers taught in the grade levels of 9th – 12th.

TABLE 11

Descriptive Statistics of Participants' Status of Receiving a Stipend

	Frequency	Percent
No	22	42.3
Yes	30	57.7
Total	52	100.0

Forty-two percent of the participants were not recipients of a stipend during the current school year and 58% of the participants were recipients of a stipend during the current school year.

Statistical Analysis

The Statistical Package for Social Science (SPSS 12.0 for Windows Student Version) was utilized to analyze the data that was collected during the study. Multiple regression analyses were utilized to examine the data. The criterion variable was teachers' perceived job satisfaction. The predictor variables were measures of teachers' perceived involvement and participation, measures of teachers' perceived motivation, level of instruction, stipend recipient, and years of teaching experience.

TABLE 12

Descriptive Statistics of the Three Measures

	Satisfaction	Motivation	Involvement
	N = 52		

Mean	69.52	168.60	67.71
Median	72.00	172.50	68.00
Mode	79	157(a)	53(a)
Std. Deviation	10.955	16.584	16.029
Range	52	74	78
Minimum	36	120	24
Maximum	88	194	102

(a) Multiple modes exist. The smallest value is shown

The criterion variable was based on the scores from the participants' responses to the Job Satisfaction Index. The range of possible scores on the index was 18 to 90. The participants' scores on the Job Satisfaction Index had a range of 52, with a minimum score of 36 and a maximum score of 88. The mean score was 69.52, the median score was 72, and the mode was 79. The standard deviation was 10.955 (see Table 12).

Two of the predictor variables were based on the scores from participants' responses to the Self-Motivation Inventory and the Teacher Involvement and Participation Scale. For the Self Motivation Inventory, the range of possible scores was from 40 to 200. The participants' scores had a range of 74, with a minimum score of 120 and a maximum score of 194. The mean score was 168.6, the median score was 172.5, and there were multiple modes, the smallest being 157. The standard deviation was 16.584 (see Table 12).

The other predictor variable was based on scores from participants' responses to the Teacher Involvement and Participation Scale. The range of possible scores for the Teacher Involvement and Participation Scales was from 22-110. The range from the actual scores of the participants was 78, with a minimum score of 24 and a maximum score of 102. The mean score was 67.71. The median score was 68. The smallest mode was 53 (see Table 12).

The multiple correlation (R), a squared multiple correlation (R^2), and an adjusted squared multiple correlation (R^2_{adj}) were utilized to complete the data analysis. Each of the three computations relay how well the predictor variables in the regression equation predict the criterion variable of teachers' perceived job satisfaction.

Therefore the function of the multiple correlation is to represent the relationship between the predicted criterion score ($\hat{Y}$) and the actual criterion score (Y). A correlation coefficient generated from the association is represented by values between the range of ± 1. $\pm$ One indicates a prefect linear relationship, and thereby the predictor variables are able to precisely predict the criterion variable. A $\pm$ value approaching 0 signifies a weakening in the relationship between the specified variables. In addition, by multiplying the squared multiple correlation (R^2) by 100%, a percentage of the variance from the criterion variable can be explained by its association to the predictor variables.

TABLE 13

Model Summary of Satisfaction and Traits

Model	R	R Square	Adjusted R Square	Std. Error of the Estimate
1	.566(a)	.321	.247	9.508

a Predictors: (Constant), Involvement, Motivation, Level, Experience, Stipend

Hypothesis One

The first research hypothesis stated that there is a statistically significant combined effect in the relationship between teachers' traits (as measures of perceived job involvement, perceived motivation, level of instruction, stipend recipient, and years of teaching experience) and the teachers' perceived job satisfaction. The results of the data analysis support the first hypothesis, there is a statistically significant combined effect on the relationship between teachers' traits (as measures of perceived job involvement, perceived motivation, level of instruction, stipend recipient, and years of teaching experience) and their perceived job satisfaction. The measures of teachers' traits are significantly related to measures of teachers' perceived job satisfaction, $R^2 = .32$, $R^2_{adj} = .24$, $F(5, 46) = 4.34$ p = .003. Thereby 32% of the variance of teachers' perceived job satisfaction can be explained by the linear relationship with the five predictor variables. A correlation coefficient matrix of the predictor variables and the criterion variables can be seen in Table 13.

TABLE 14

Correlation Coefficients of Satisfaction and Traits

		Satisfaction	Experience	Level	Stipend	Motivation	Involvement
				Participants (N = 52)			
Pearson Correlation	Satisfaction		-.095	-.127	.285*	.092	.500***
	Experience	-.095		-.029	.039	.217	.198
	Level	-.127	-.029		.014	.192	-.174
	Stipend	.285*	.039	.014		.071	.379**
	Motivation	.092	.217	.192	.071		.006
	Involvement	.500***	.198	-.174	.379**	.006	

*Significant at p < .05, **Significant at p < .01, ***Significant at p < .001

Hypothesis Two

The second research hypothesis stated that measures of teachers' perceived motivation have the highest correlation with the teachers' perceived job satisfaction. In order to test this hypothesis the relationship between each predictor variable and teachers' perceived job satisfaction was examined.

The relationship between teachers' perceived motivation and teachers' perceived job satisfaction was .092 p < .258, which was not significant and did not support the hypothesis. The relationship between teachers' perceived job involvement and participation and teachers' perceived job satisfaction was .50, p < .001, which was significant; however did not support the hypothesis. The relationship between level of instruction and teachers' perceived job satisfaction was -.127 p < .185. This relationship was not significant and did not support the hypothesis. The relationship between stipend recipient and teachers' perceived job satisfaction was .285 p < .020. The relationship was significant and did not support the hypothesis. The relationship between teachers' years of teaching experience and job satisfaction was -.095 p < .251. The relationship was not significant and did not support the hypothesis. The results for this analysis can be seen in Table 13.

TABLE 15

Model Summary Motivation and Involvement

Model	R	R Square	Adjusted R Square	Std. Error of the Estimate	Change Statistics				
					R Square Change	F Change	df1	df2	Sig. F Change
1	.508(a)	.258	.228	9.627	.258	8.522	2	49	.001
2	.566(b)	.321	.247	9.508	.062	1.410	3	46	.252

a. Predictors: (Constant), Involvement, Motivation

b. Predictors: (Constant), Involvement, Motivation, Level, Experience, Stipend

Hypothesis Three

The third research hypothesis stated that measures of teachers' perceived traits will be statistically greater than the actual traits of the teachers. The multiple regression analysis model for two-ordered sets was utilized to answer question three. The procedure is quite similar to a one set multiple linear regression analysis, however the teachers' traits were divided into two sets. One set was the measures of teachers' perceived traits, which included measures of teachers' perceived involvement and participation, and measures of teachers' perceived motivation (Set 1). The next set included actual traits, which were the teachers' level of instruction, stipend recipient, and years of teaching experience (Set 2). The analysis of the two-ordered set addressed the research question with the computation of the R^2 change.

The results of the third hypothesis test, measures of teachers' perceived traits will be statistically greater than the actual traits of the teachers, was significant, $R^2 = .258$, $R^2_{adj} = .228$, $F(2, 49) = .8.52$, $p < .001$. The measures of the actual traits did not significantly predict over and above the perceived traits, R^2 change = .06, $F(3, 46) = 1.41$, $p = .252$. The results suggest that the actual traits of teachers did not improve the ability to predict teachers' job satisfaction. The results can be seen in Table 15.

An additional significant finding found among the correlation coefficients in the matrix was the coefficient produced from the relationship between teachers' perceived involvement and participation and the stipend recipient during the current school year, .379 $p < .003$.

TABLE 16

Coefficients(a) of Satisfaction and Traits

Model		Unstandardized Coefficients		Standardized Coefficients	Correlations		
		B	Std. Error	Beta	Zero-order	Partial	Part
1	(Constant)	32.996	14.901				

Experience	-1.446	.796	-.231	-.095	-.259	-.221
Grade	-.983	1.609	-.077	-.127	-.090	-.074
Stipend	2.125	2.905	.097	.285	.107	.089
Motivation	.097	.084	.147	.092	.168	.140
Involvement	.338	.093	.495	.500	.471	.440

a: Dependent Variable: Satisfaction

The zero order correlation, which is also known as a bivariate correlation, is present in Table 16. Through statistical analysis, the effect of the additional predictor variables can be partialled out from the effects on the criterion and the predictor variable, this computation in Table 16 can be found under partial. A slightly different correlation, the part correlation, only controls the affect of the other predictor variables on the specified predictor variable, but not the criterion variable.

A predicted variable ($\hat{Y}$) is produced from the predictor variables that are involved in a linear regression equation. $B_1 - B_5$ served as the slope weights and $X_1 - X_5$ respectively served as the predictor variables in the linear regression equation, and the last element of the equation, B_0, is the constant, which is courtesy of the criterion variable. In this study there were five predictor variables, thereby creating a regression equation of: $Y = B_1X_1 = B_2X_2 + B_3X_3 + B_4X_4 + B_5X_5 + B_0$.

According to the B weights that were generated the linear regression equation is: *Predicted Job Satisfaction* = .09 *Motivation* + .33 *Involvement* - .98 *Grade* + 2.12 *Stipend* − 1.44 *Experience* + 32.99 *(Constant)*. To assist in the statistical analysis the independent and dependent variables were standardized, thereby creating a mean of 0 and a standard deviation of 1. According to the standardized weights the linear equation is: Z *predicted job satisfaction* = ⁻.23 *Experience* ⁻.07 *Grade* + .09 *Stipend* + .14 *Motivation* + .49 *Involvement*

Summary

This chapter reported the findings of the data analysis of the data collected during the study. The criterion variable was teachers' perceived job satisfaction. The predictor variables were measures of teachers' perceived involvement and participation, teachers' perceived motivation, level of instruction, stipend recipient, and years of teaching experience. The predictor variables were able to predict a portion of the variability that exists in the teachers' perceived job satisfaction, $R^2 = .32$, $R^2_{adj} = .24$, $F(5, 46) = 4.34$ $p = .003$. Thereby 32% of the variance of teachers' perceived job satisfaction can be explained by the linear relationship with the five-predictor variables. Individually only two of the measures were statistically significantly related to teachers' perceived job satisfaction: (a) the relationship with the measures of teachers' perceived involvement and participation, .50, $p < .001$, and (b) the relationship with teachers who receive a stipend, .379, $p = .003$. The results of hypothesis three, teachers' perceived traits will be statistically greater than the actual traits of the teachers, was significant, $R^2 = .258$, $R^2_{adj} = .228$, $F(2, 49) = .8.52$, $p < .001$. The measures of the actual traits did not significantly predict over and above the perceived traits, R^2 change $= .06$, $F(3, 46) = 1.41$, $p = .252$.

CHAPTER FIVE

Discussion

The previous chapter reviewed the findings from the analyses of the data collected during this study. The purpose of this study was to describe the extent to which the specified factors predicted teachers' perceived job satisfaction. The data analysis was completed by utilizing multiple regression statistical procedures. The criterion variable was job satisfaction and the predictor variables were measures of teachers' perceived involvement and participation, measures of teachers' perceived motivation, level of instruction, stipend recipient, and years of teaching experience. The data were collected from 52 teachers in the Houston Independent School District. This chapter discusses the findings of the study and elaborates on the significance, implications, recommendations, and concludes with a summary.

The first research hypothesis stated that there is a statistically significant combined effect in the relationship between teachers' traits (as measures of perceived job involvement, perceived motivation, level of instruction, stipend recipient, and years of teaching experience) and their job satisfaction. The results and previous research supported the hypothesis. Teachers' traits explain 32% of the variance that exists with the teachers' perceived job satisfaction. Of the five-predictor variables, two variables significantly accounted for most of the variance observed in the linear relationship between the predictor variables and teachers' perceived job satisfaction. The two predictor variables that accounted for the most variance are teachers' perceived involvement and participation and stipend recipient. The relationship lends itself to the contention that teachers are willing and satisfied with increased participation in school related activities, in addition to teaching a full course load, if they are compensated above their base salary. In this case, compensation came in the form of a stipend.

The second research hypothesis stated the measures of teachers' perceived motivation have the highest correlation with teachers' perceived job satisfaction. To validate the hypotheses the strength and direction of each coefficient is discussed to determine which predictor variable has the highest correlation to teachers' perceived job satisfaction.

The first predictor variable reviewed was teachers' perceived motivation. The individual effect of perceived motivation on teachers' perceived job satisfaction was not found to be significant $r = .092$ $p < .258$. The strength of the relationship was lower than expected, and the results did not support the hypothesis. The non-significant finding was not expected because the research states that individuals who have high motivation are more likely to experience high job satisfaction (Herzberg, 1962). Several factors may have attributed to the non-significant finding between teachers' perceived motivation and teachers' perceived job satisfaction. Some of the factors include, but are not limited to: faults within the survey, limited response rate, and the self-reports.

The Self-Motivation Inventory intended to measure one's perceived motivation to determine if teachers' who possessed high motivation experienced high job satisfaction. It is difficult to define each facet within the construct of motivation, and even more difficult to measure the true representation of motivation in individuals. Motivator factors have the ability to allow individuals to demonstrate their abilities and thereby witness their growth achieved through their efforts. The survey deployed its best efforts to measure motivation; however, it did not capture the true essence of what was intended to be measured such as one's perceptions of motivations in regards to "achievement, recognition, work itself, responsibility, and advancement" (Herzberg, 1962, p. 77).

There was an adequate amount of teachers in the sample that were requested to participate in the study; 19% of the teachers in the sample chose to participate in the study, and 81% chose not to participate in the study. The participants of the study were volunteers, and research shows that there are differences between individuals that choose to participate and those who choose not to participate. The surveys utilized in the study were self-administered, and the participants may have misinterpreted various items. Moreover, the responses to the items in the surveys were self-reported by the participants; therefore, the items are only as accurate as reported by the participants.

When reviewing the three correlations in the correlation matrix in Table 16 the non-zero (bivariate) relationship was reported as $r = .092$. While the partial correlation, which controls for the other predictor variables influence on both the predictor variable in question, motivation, and the criterion variable, job satisfaction, was $r = .168$. Thereafter, the part correlation controls for the other predictor variables affect on the motivation, but not on the teachers' perceived job satisfaction. This weakened the relationship between teachers' perceived motivation and teachers' perceived job satisfaction to $r = .140$. These results suggest partialling out the affect on both the criterion and predictor variables improves the relationship between teachers' perceived motivation and teachers' perceived job satisfaction the most ($r = .168$). Thereafter, only controlling for the affect of the other variables on the predictor variable of motivation, and not the criterion variable weakens the relationship to $r = .140$; however this relationship is still stronger than the non-zero correlation that does not control for the other predictor variables at all, which further diminishes the relationship to $r = .092$. The results suggest that the other predictor variables in this study reduce the significance of the relationship between teachers' perceived motivation and teachers' perceived job satisfaction. Although the other predictor variables did not function to strengthen the relationship between teachers' perceived motivation and teachers' perceived job satisfaction, there may be other variables that enhance the relationship of these two variables.

The relationship between teachers' perceived motivation and teachers' perceived job satisfaction was expected to be the highest. The weak relationship found may be explained by a series of occurrences, such as unpredictable extraneous variables that eventually diminish any form of a relationship between the two variables of teachers' perceived motivation and teachers' perceived job satisfaction. Hypothetically, an individual may start with high motivation, which would justify the expenditure of extra effort to reach a goal. Upon reaching the goal, satisfaction would ensue. However, often factors prevent goals from being attained. One may have high motivation, but never reach the goal, and therefore never achieve satisfaction. The literature contends that motivation is the driving force behind every action (Herzberg, 1959). The drive towards accomplishing the goal is courtesy of motivation. However, when one reaches the goal, and is then satisfied, motivation may be reduced or become non-existent. Because the relationship between teachers' perceived motivation and teachers' perceived job satisfaction constantly changes, it may be difficult to observe a relationship that is not abstract. Nonetheless, the relationship between teachers' perceived motivation and teachers' perceived job satisfaction was not found to be significant.

The hypothesis stated that the best individual predictor of teachers' perceived job satisfaction is teachers' perceived motivation. The literature supports the hypothesis; however, the results do not support the hypothesis. The best individual predictor of job satisfaction was teachers' perceived involvement and participation. The coefficient r = .50 accounts for a portion of the variance that exists in the linear relationship with job satisfaction. In reviewing the correlation matrix, it appears as though the other variables diminished the relationship between teachers' perceived participation and involvement and teachers' perceived job satisfaction. The partial correlation, which controls the other predictor variables influence on teachers' perceived involvement and participation and teachers' job satisfaction, was r = .471. The part correlation, which controls for the predictor variables influence on teachers' perceived involvement and participation, but not on teachers' perceived job satisfaction, was r = .440.

It is logical to fathom that by teachers participating in activities that are of interest to them that an increase in job satisfaction would ensue. Professional learning communities are a forum that allows teachers to engage in meaningful exchanges, which may not only enhance their professional relationships, but also provide enhanced strategies to their repertoire of teaching tools (DuFour, et. al, 2002). Teachers equipped with additional knowledge of strategies, content areas, and student learning are better able to meet the demands of the job and assist in making positive gains in the academic achievement of students. When teachers expand their jobs to include areas outside of the teaching domain they may avoid stagnation and engage in stimulating activity. Teachers who have the opportunity to participate in various clubs, committees, and discussions may gain substantial benefits to their ways of thinking and planning. In contrast, to the teachers who experience high involvement and participation, there are the teachers who may not want to participate because they feel burnt-out. Teachers who experience isolation and lack of collegiate support may have stifled creativity. Teachers may not be aware of the job satisfaction that awaits them should they partake in additional involvement endeavors such as professional learning communities. These teachers may be leery of the perceived burden of the involvement and participation in professional learning communities. The best approach to entice teachers into professional learning communities may be to allow the promising and exciting news of the participants to filter out to the non-participants. The literature states after the implementation of a professional learning communities often a new culture will replace the traditional culture and there may be increases in: (a) teachers' collegiality, (b) teachers' enthusiasm, (c) exchanges of dialogue among teachers, (d) teachers' job satisfaction, and (e) student achievement (Strahan, 2002).

The next relationship explored was the relationship between level of instruction and job satisfaction. There are many observable differences in the characteristics of teachers of different levels of instruction. Level of instruction was added to determine if it significantly improved the set of predictor variables, known as traits, ability to predict job satisfaction and to determine if there was a significant relationship between teachers' level of instruction and teachers' perceived job satisfaction. A strong relationship between the higher levels of instruction and job satisfaction or a strong relationship between lower grade levels of instruction and job satisfaction was reasonable to expect, however this was not the case. The relationship between level of instruction and job satisfaction was not significant $r = -.127$ $p < .185$, which did not support the hypothesis. This weak relationship suggests that as satisfaction increases, level of instruction decreases. Thereby supporting the contention that as job satisfaction decreases, the level of instruction increases. The relationship of level of instruction and job satisfaction is influenced by other variables. This can be observed by controlling for the effects of the predictor variables on both level of instruction and job satisfaction in what is known as a partial correlation. The result of the partial correlation was r = -.090. The part correlation controls for the other predictor variables affect on the level of instruction, but not teachers' perceived job satisfaction. The result of the part correlation was r = -.074.

Stipend recipient was found to be significantly associated to job satisfaction r = .285 p < .020. The other predictor variables of the study diminish the relationship between stipend recipient and teachers' perceived job satisfaction. From partialling out the affect of the other predictor variables on stipend recipient and teachers' perceived job satisfaction the magnitude of the relationship was reduced, the partial correlation was r = .107. The result from the part correlation, where the affects of the other predictor variables were controlled for on the predictor variable of stipend recipient, but not on the criterion variable of job satisfaction, the correlation was r = .089.

Stipends are a form of compensation. The purpose of compensation is to reward one for his or her valued efforts. The mere fact that one is receiving a token of recognition may function to ignite feelings of job satisfaction. Stipends may also serve as a form of self-validation of well-applied efforts. In addition, stipends may be the monetary supplement that makes the job of teaching worthwhile to some teachers. Many teachers contend that they are not adequately paid; receiving a stipend may be just the cure for the perception of an inadequate paycheck. In addition, some teachers may view their job as strictly teaching, and anything above teaching should qualify for additional pay. Teachers who believe that they are entitled to additional compensation and who do not receive it, may experience reduced job satisfaction or increased dissatisfaction because of the inequality of one's efforts (output) and what is being received (input) (Herzberg, 1959; Dessler, 1999).

The last predictor variable to be examined was years of teaching experience as it relates to job satisfaction. Although years of teaching experience was not selected to be the best predictor of job satisfaction, it was reasonable to expect that a relationship did exist between the two variables. The predictor variable of years of teaching experience and teachers' perceived job satisfaction, was $r = -.095$ $p < .251$, the relationship was not significant, which did not support the hypothesis. In reviewing the correlation of teachers' years of teaching experience and teachers' perceived job satisfaction, it appears as though the other predictor variables significantly enhanced the magnitude of the relationship between teachers' years of teaching experience and teachers' perceived job satisfaction. The partial correlation, which controls for the affect of the other predictor variables on the predictor variable of years of teaching experience and the criterion variable of job satisfaction, was $r = -.259$. The part correlation, which only controls for other predictor variables affect on years of teaching experience, was $r = -.221$.

Teachers have first hand knowledge of what has previously worked with their students (Lambert, 2002). Through years of experience, it is plausible that teachers have remained in the field of teaching because of their fondness and affinity for teaching. This fondness may be seen as a strong correlation between years of teaching experience and teachers' perceived job satisfaction; however, this was not found to be so. Another factor that may influence teachers' decisions to remain in the field of education that does not support an association to job satisfaction is their retirement plan (Dworkin, 1987). Teachers' retirement plans continue to improve through the length of time that is invested in their teaching career. Therefore, teachers who want to reap the benefits of a good retirement plan remain in the field of teaching against their desires to placate their need for job satisfaction. Retirement plans may actually work against teachers' ability to achieve job satisfaction by binding them to a career, which is no longer their interest. The results of the analysis between teachers' years of experience in association to job satisfaction found that as years of experience increase, job satisfaction decreases. This finding suggests that teachers come into the field of teaching invigorated and satisfied with their decision to teach, however, through time their level of satisfaction diminishes and they find themselves bound to their career.

The third research hypothesis stated the measures of teachers' perceived traits will be statistically greater than the actual traits of the teachers. The perceived traits accounted for 26% of the variance with job satisfaction. Essentially, teachers' perceived involvement and participation accounted for 25% and teachers' perceived motivation accounted for 1% thereby totaling 26%. The perceived traits were better able to predict job satisfaction over and above the actual traits. The actual traits included level of instruction, stipend recipient, and years of teaching experience; this set of predictor variables was not able to explain a significant portion of the variance over and above the variance that was explained by the perceived traits, which was noted by the insignificant R^2 change of .062.

Significant Finding

The criterion variable of the study was job satisfaction. It is important to understand the variables that are able to predict job satisfaction because studies have shown that satisfied employees tend to remain with their employer for extended periods. In addition, satisfied employees also have improved job performance, for teachers this may mean enhanced instructional delivery to students. When teachers experience a lack of job satisfaction, they may discontinue their employment in the field of education (Community Banker, 2001). Teacher attrition is a massive concern that many schools and school districts are facing (Ballinger, 2000).

After reviewing the literature, several factors were identified as key components to the job satisfaction of teachers. These factors were motivation, teacher involvement, and stipend recipient. These factors assisted in formulating the first research question and hypothesis. The first research hypothesis stated that there is a statistically significant combined effect in the relationship between teachers' traits (as measures of perceived job involvement, perceived motivation, level of instruction, stipend recipient, and years of teaching experience) and their job satisfaction. The analysis of the data collected during this study found several significant findings. The findings of the first analysis states that 32% of the variance that exist in job satisfaction can be explained by the predictor variables of teachers' traits. Explaining the variance that exists with the job satisfaction of teachers is important because the research suggests that satisfied workers are productive workers. Although there is a significant amount of variance that is unaccounted for, 32% is a good start to improving the working conditions and atmosphere of teachers, which ultimately affects the quality of instruction delivered to students (Chan, Gee, & Steiner; 2000).

The second research hypothesis stated the measures of teachers' perceived motivation have the highest correlation with the job satisfaction of teachers. The individual effect of each predictor variable on job satisfaction was evaluated to determine which variable was able to individually predict job satisfaction the best. Identifying the variables that predict job satisfaction is important to the development of teachers and students. Implemented correctly, the variables may increase teachers' perceived job satisfaction, and thereby, the students may reap the rewards.

Teachers' perceived motivation was the first predictor variable examined. The results found a correlation of r = .092 p < .258 between teachers' perceived motivation and job satisfaction. The finding of the data analysis was not significant. Motivation can be an internal drive or an external object. Teachers were prompted to report about their general sentiments and behavior regarding motivation when faced with arbitrary situations. Each person has characteristics that are descriptive of him or her, and thereby allow the person to generalize from previously exhibited and experienced sentiments and behaviors. However, specific tasks were not identified and this may have reduced the teachers' ability to report their motivation. A stronger relationship was produced between stipend recipients and teachers' perceived job satisfaction, which supports this contention. The measurement of stipend recipient was concrete, in contrast to the measurement of teachers' perceived motivation. It was not presented as a question of if the participant had received a token of appreciation, but did the participant receive a stipend, which not only identifies the object in question, but also verifies the receipt of the object. A significant relationship was found, r = .285, p = .020. The abstract nature of the teachers' perceptions of motivation may have been a factor why the relationship with teachers' perceived job satisfaction was not significant.

Teachers' perceived job involvement and participation was the next predictor variable examined. There was a correlation of r = .50, p < .001 found in the association between teachers' perceived job involvement and teachers' perceived job satisfaction.

This finding is important because teachers' involvement and participation is a significant component of professional learning communities. The literature contends that teachers in professional learning communities exchange and create ideas that may significantly improve their instructional endeavors and thereby increase the academic achievement of students (LaFee, 2003). In addition, professional learning communities contend that teachers experience increased satisfaction through shared dialogues and interaction with peers to create energized plans and strategies for the academic progression of student achievement (DuFour, et. al, 2002; Lambert, 2002).

Level of instruction was another predictor variable of the study examined. The results found a correlation of $r = -.127$, $p < .185$, between the level of instruction and teachers' perceived job satisfaction. The relationship was not found to be significant.

Stipend recipient was the next predictor variable examined. The results found a correlation of $r = .285$, $p < .020$, in the relationship between stipend recipient and teachers' perceived job satisfaction. This relationship is important because it suggests that teachers value stipends. The value that teachers place on stipends may be a factor influencing their job satisfaction. In addition, receiving a stipend may provide a form of validation to teachers, thereby increasing their self-worth (Enderlin-Lampe, 2002).

Lastly, the predictor variable of teachers' years of teaching experience was examined. The results found a correlation of $r = -.095$, $p < .251$, between teachers' years of teaching experience and teachers' perceived job satisfaction. This finding was not significant.

A significant finding was found in the data analysis between teachers' perceived involvement and stipend recipient $r = .379$, $p < .003$. This finding is noteworthy because it suggests that involvement and participation may increase when teachers receive a stipend for their efforts. Realizing the goals that have been set for students is an immense responsibility; however the results of this study suggest that teachers are willing to provide the supplementary effort needed to improve student achievement when compensated by a stipend.

An investment in teachers may be viewed in terms of a tree in nature. Although a tree may require water, it provides so much more than the mere investment of water such as shade, fruit, leaves, branches, as do teachers. Society is very apprehensive about any investment that is not directly related to students, and therefore many areas in education have been neglected, the most devastating is the teacher. An investment in improving the conditions surrounding teachers may have tremendous ameliorating effects to the lives and education of students. From enhancing the conditions that affect teachers, the whole school may become stronger and experience improvements (Choy, 1996).

Implications

The findings of this study have developed into implication that may potentially be very beneficial for not only teachers, but students as well. The first research hypothesis stated that there is a statistically significant combined effect in the relationship between teachers' traits (as measures of perceived job involvement, perceived motivation, level of instruction, stipend recipient, and years of teaching experience) and their job satisfaction. The findings of the analysis state that 32% of the variance of job satisfaction can be explained by its linear relationship with the predictor variables of teachers' traits. Because 32% of the variance of job satisfaction can be explained, measures should be taken to implement the conditions that have been found as a source of job satisfaction for teachers.

The second research hypothesis stated the measures of teachers' perceived motivation have the highest correlation with the job satisfaction of teachers. The individual effect of each predictor variable on job satisfaction was evaluated to determine which variable was able to predict job satisfaction the best.

Teachers' perceived motivation was the first predictor variable examined. The results found a correlation of $r = .092$, $p < .258$, between teachers' perceived motivation and teachers' perceived job satisfaction. The literature contends motivation is important, however implications from the results suggest considerable efforts should not be utilized to gain the interest of teachers (Herzberg, 1959). Other literature and the results from the study suggest that involving teachers in professional learning communities would be a better employment of effort (LaFee, 2003).

Teachers' perceived job involvement and participation was the next predictor variable examined. There was a correlation of $r = .50$, $p < .001$ found in the relationship of teachers' perceived job involvement and teachers' perceived job satisfaction. The implication of the finding is that schools and school administrators interested in making improvements should take steps to increase teachers' involvement and participation in the areas of their interest. Participation may diversify the job of teachers and lead to increased job satisfaction. Research by Argyris, Likert, & McGregor found that employees like variation and being challenged, and teachers' jobs may be too routinized to peak or maintain their satisfaction (Lawler, 1986). Expanded opportunities may explain part of the reason why teachers who participate in other work related tasks outside of the classroom experience increased job satisfaction.

Level of instruction was another predictor variable examined. The results found a correlation of $r = -.127$, $p < .185$, between the level of instruction and teachers' perceived job satisfaction. There are not any implications that have resulted from this finding.

Stipend recipient was the next predictor variable examined. The results found a correlation of $r = .285$, $p < .020$, in the relationship between stipend recipient and teachers' perceived job satisfaction. The implications from the findings suggest that teachers value the receipt of stipends. The results also suggest that teachers who receive stipends are more satisfied with their jobs. In addition, the finding suggests that teachers are more likely to be involved and participate if they receive a stipend. Therefore, schools and school districts should investigate and invest in additional avenues to provide teachers with stipends for their additional efforts.

Lastly, the predictor variable of teachers' years of teaching experience was examined. The results found a correlation of $r = -.095$, $p < .251$, between teachers' years of teaching experience and teachers' perceived job satisfaction. There are no implications as a result of this finding.

The academic achievement of students throughout the world is under increased scrutiny. School districts across the United States are trying to implement initiatives and strategies that will increase the academic achievement of students. In the hustle to implement the best practices in regards to the instruction of students, the overall maintenance of teachers' job satisfaction has been neglected. It is important to the academic development of students to ensure that teachers are satisfied and motivated in regards to their job so that they will put forth the required effort that will facilitate students reaching their highest potential (Kelley & Odden, 1995). The results of the study suggest that compensating teachers with stipends and encouraging their involvement and participation is associated to job satisfaction.

Recommendations

Improving students' academic achievement is one of the main goals of education. It is important that resources are optimized to realize this goal. Teachers have the immense responsibility of achieving this goal for hundreds to thousands of students during a career in education. It is essential to the progress and academic well-being of students that teachers are provided with the working conditions and the environment that will enhance their ability to teach.

The review of the literature and the findings of this limited research study generated information that has culminated into practical recommendations and recommendations for future lines of research. The recommendations for future lines of research may provide further developments to the body of knowledge concerning improvement to teachers' satisfaction and working conditions that may improve teachers' ability to instruct students. The practical recommendations may be implemented immediately with teachers to enhance their teaching careers, and facilitate improvements in the academic achievement of students. The three practical recommendations from the review of the literature and the findings of this research study are:

1. Increase the involvement and participation of teachers.

2. Establish professional learning communities for teachers.

3. Increase the use of stipends distributed to teachers for their additional efforts.

The findings from this research study and the review of the literature suggest that teachers who are involved and participate in school related functions in addition to their duties as a classroom teacher, experience increased satisfaction. Therefore, schools and school districts should take immediate measures to increase teachers' collective participation in school decision making including but not limited to: (a) administration, (b) student discipline, (c) curriculum development, and (d) the school budget. Increasing teachers' involvement and participation in school related activities, beyond instructing students may improve and strengthen teachers' relationships and interactions with students, colleagues, and administrators; and invigorate their interest in teaching.

Next, schools and school districts should take measures to establish forums such as professional learning communities where teachers can engage in thought provoking exchanges that may enhance their ability to instruct students. Professional learning communities provide teachers with many amenities that support and strengthen teachers holistically. The amenities of professional learning communities include (a) enhancing teachers' knowledge of students' learning styles, (b) providing information on innovative research that may stimulate teachers and students, and (c) creating support systems for teachers.

In addition to increasing the involvement and participation of teachers and establishing professional learning communities, schools and school districts should take measures to compensate teachers with stipends for their additional efforts outside of the classroom when possible. The review of literature and the findings from this research study suggest that teachers are interested in stipends and have increased satisfaction when compensated for their efforts in the form of a stipend. Stipends function to enhance the satisfaction of teachers by demonstrating the teacher is valued, and by providing teachers with their highly sought after additional income.

Job satisfaction is a dominant factor affecting teachers. It affects teachers' behavior and ability to carryout daily procedures and instruction. It is important to the longevity of a teacher's career and performance that optimal job satisfaction is achieved. The recommendations for future lines of research were generated from reviewing the findings from this study and the review of the literature.

It may be beneficial to conduct a regression analysis on the effect of teachers' work related tasks, including but not limited to: (a) whole group instruction, (b) one-on-one tutoring, (c) small group facilitation, (d) mentoring, (e) school budgeting, and (f) curriculum planning; on their job satisfaction. From the regression analysis, the combined and individual effects of work related tasks on teachers' job satisfaction can be examined to possibly improve teachers' working conditions, and thereby improve their ability to be effective instructional providers, and improve student achievement.

It may be beneficial for researchers to examine additional predictor variables that may strengthen the ability to predict teachers' job satisfaction. This would thereby allow schools to better understand the conditions that would optimize teachers' job satisfaction. When teachers experience high job satisfaction, their performance is enhanced. Students are the recipients of teachers' enhanced job performance, which is essential and beneficial to the academic achievement and educational progression of students.

Teachers have increasing responsibilities from year to year. A correlation of r = .379 was found between teachers' perceived involvement and participation, and stipend recipient; however, the teachers' perceived involvement was not expressly explicit (was the involvement for a stipend paid activity or a non-stipend paid activity). Additional research is needed to clarify whether teachers are compensated with a stipend for their involvement and participation or do they participate under voluntary non-paid conditions.

Additional research is needed on teachers' job involvement and participation to determine if teachers: (a) value greater variation in their job, (b) value participating in school decision-making, or (c) participate outside of the classroom strictly because of monetary gain. There may be any number of reasons that drive teachers' involvement and participation in school related functions outside of the classroom; nonetheless, efforts should be applied to evaluate the primary reasons that teachers are involved and participate in various non-required work related activities. In addition, further research is needed to describe the nature of the relationship among (a) student performance, (b) academic achievement, and (c) the job satisfaction of teachers.

The field of education may improve by analyzing the instructional qualities and characteristics of teachers whose students display high growth and high academic achievement. Thereafter researchers may attempt to replicate the conditions to attain high academic growth and achievement for all students.

There are a myriad of stipends distributed in school districts. Stipends can range from 25 to 20,000 USD. The field of education may benefit from additional research on the predictive capabilities of stipends and their respective amounts on both the job satisfaction and the job involvement of teachers (HISD, 2004).

Additional research may also be beneficial in regards to stipends to determine the underlying contention of stipends. Do teachers value stipends strictly for their monetary value or is it the gesture of appreciation for their efforts? In addition, if teachers' value of stipends is purely based on a token of appreciation, would teachers be as receptive to other items as tokens of appreciation?

Surveys are widely used in research to collect data from participants. However, there are various problems associated with the self-administration of surveys with the participants in studies. Therefore, in future studies researchers should add an observation component in addition to the self-reports of the participants as to verify and validate the self-reports of the participants.

Summary

Teachers are a significant component of the system of education. It is important to take into consideration the factors that affect the job satisfaction of teachers. Many variables may increase or reduce the job satisfaction of teachers. While it is impossible to establish ideal working conditions for teachers, efforts can be implemented to foster the conditions associated with teachers who experience high job satisfaction.

Several significant findings were generated from the multiple regression analysis done from on the data collected in this study. Thirty-two percent of the variance of job satisfaction can be explained by its linear relationship with the predictor variables. The next significant finding was the association between teachers' perceived job satisfaction and stipend recipient, $r = .285$. The next noteworthy finding was the association between teacher involvement and participation, and stipend recipient, $r = .379$. These findings are important because they may assist in improving the work conditions of teachers, which may enhance their ability to instruct students. The implications produced from this study revolve around improving job satisfaction and the academic achievement of students by utilizing professional learning communities to increase job involvement, and apply stipends to further these two goals. Further study is needed to make continued advancements in the field of education.

References

Abel, M. & Sewell, J. (1992). Stress and burnout in rural and urban secondary school teachers. *Journal of Educational Research, 92,* 287-311.

American Psychological Association. (2001). Publication Manual (5th ed.) Washington, DC.

Anderman, E. Bleazer, & Smith (1991). *Teacher commitment and job satisfaction: The role of school culture and principal leadership.* (Report No. EA 026 201). Urbana, IL: Educational Management. (Eric Document Reproduction Service No. ED 375497)

Axtell, C. M., & Parker, S. K. (2003). Promoting role breadth self-efficacy through involvement, work redesign, and training. *Human Relations, 56*(1), 113-131.

Ballinger, J. (2000). Programs aim to stop teacher washout. *Journal of Staff Development, 21*(2), 1-8. Retrieved February 5, 2002, from http://www.nsdc.org/library/jsd/ballinger212.html.

Bandura, A. (1994). *Self-efficacy.* In V.S. Ramachaudran (ed.) encyclopedia of human behavior, 4, 71-81). San Diego: New York Academic Press. (Reprinted in H. Friedman [Ed.], Encyclopedia of Mental Health, 1998.

Bandura. A. (1977). Self-efficacy: Toward unifying theory of behavioral change. *Psychology Review, 84*, 191-215.

Bentacourt-Smith, M., Iman D. & Marlow, L. (1994). *Professional attrition: An examination of minority and non-minority teachers at-risk.* (Report No. SP 036285) Nashville, Tennessee: Annual Meeting Mid-South Educational Research Association. (Eric Document Reproduction Service No. ED 388639)

Biggs, J. B. (1989). Approaches to the enhancement of teaching, *Higher Education Research and Development, 8,* 7-25.

Bishop, L. J. (1977). *Visualizing a staff development plan.* In C. W. Beegle & R. A. Edelfelt (Eds.). Staff development / staff liberation (p. 52-59). Washington, DC: Association of Supervision and Curriculum Development.

Boyd, B. (1993). *Transforming teacher staff development.* (Report No. EA 025 253) Colorado: Educational Management. (ERIC Documentation Reproductive Service No. ED 362943)

Bozionelos, N. (2004). The big five of personality and work involvement. *Journal of Managerial Psychology, 19*(1), 69-81.

Bredson & Scribner (2000). A statewide professional development conference: Useful strategy for learning or inefficient use of resources? *The Education Policy Analysis Archives, 8,* 13.

Brimm, J. & Tollett, D. (1974). How do teachers feel about in-service education? *Educational Leadership, 31*(6), 521-525.

Brown, K. (2002). *Labor relations. Tends and issues.* (Report No. EA 032326) Oregon: Office of Educational Research and Improvement. (ERIC Documentation Reproductive Service No. ED 472991)

Burr, R. & Cordery, J. L. (2001). Self-management efficacy as a mediator of the relation between job design and employee motivation. *Human Performance, 14*(1), 27-44.

Caffarella, R. S. (1988). *Program development and evaluation resource book for educators*. New York: John Wiley and Sons.

Chan, K. Gee, M. & Steiner, T. (2000). Employee happiness and corporate financial performance. *Financial Practice & Education, 10*, 47.

Chen, D. (2002, Fall). Exploring the precursors to teacher empowerment: Evolving thoughts. *The Delta Kappa Gamma Bulletin, 69*(1) 52-55.

Clark, D. L., Lotto, L. S. & Astuto, T. A. (1984). Effective schools and school improvement: A comparative analysis of two lines of inquiry. *Education Administration Quarterly, 20*, 41-68.

Clark, R.J., & Sideman, E. (1980). Individual imperatives in institutional self-development. *Peabody Journal of Education, 58*, 34-38.

Community Banker. (2001). *What drives employee satisfaction, 10*, 42.

Choy, S. (1996). *Teachers' working conditions*. Findings from "The Condition of Education, 1996," No. 7 (Report No. ISBN-0-16-048969-S) Washington DC: National Center for Education Statistics. (ERIC Documentation Reproductive Service No. ED 406348)

Conger, J. A. & Kanungo, R. N. (1988). The empowerment process: Integrating theory and practice. *Academy of Management Review, 13*(3), 471-482.

Cornette, L. & Gaines, G. (2002). *Quality teaching: Can incentive policies make a difference?* (Report No. SP 040 701). Atlanta, Georgia: Southern Regional Education Board. (ERIC Documentation Reproductive Service No. ED 464085)

Corwin, J. (2001). The importance of teacher morale in combating teacher shortage *Baylor Business Review, 19*, 18.

Dale, E. L. (1983). What is staff development? *Educational Leadership, 40*(1), 31.

Davis, J. & Wilson, S. (2000, July/August). *Principals' efforts to empower to teachers: Effects on teacher motivation and job satisfaction and stress.* The Clearing House, 349-353.

Dessler, G. (1999). *Human performance: Improving behavior at work.* Reston, Virginia: Reston Publishing Company, Inc.

Dinham, S. (1994). *Enhancing the quality of teacher satisfaction* (Report No. SP 035 719). Launceston, Tasmania, Australia: Australian College of Education. (ERIC Document Reproduction Service No. ED 380409)

Dishman, R. K. & Getteman, L. R. (1980) Psychobiotic influences on exercise adherence. *Journal of Sport Psychology, 2,* 295-310.

DuFour, R., Guidice, A. Magee, D., Martin, P, & Zivkovic, B. (2002). *The student support team as a professional learning community.* (Report No. EA 031 690). Illinois: Counseling and Student Services. (ERIC Documentation Reproductive Service No. ED 3464270)

Dworkin, A.G. (1987). *Teacher burnout in the public schools.* Albany, New York: SUNY Press.

Enderlin-Lampe (2002, Spring). Empowerment: Teacher perceptions, aspirations and efficacy. *Journal of Instructional Psychology 29*(3), 139-46.

Evertson, C. M. (1986). Do teachers make a difference? Issues for the eighties. *Education and Urban Society, 18*(2), 195-210.

Farnsworth, V. (2002). *Supporting professional development and teachers for understanding – Actions for administrators.* (Report No. SE 067061). Madison WI: Consortium for Research in Education. (ERIC Documentation Reproductive Service No. ED 470964)

Findings from the Condition of Education. (1996). *Teachers' working conditions.* Retrieved February 6, 2002, from http://nces.ed.gov/pubs97/97371.htm

Fiske, E. B. (1983, October 4). *Teacher fulfillment put above pay.* The New York Times. CIO.

Ford, C. M. (1999, September). Interpretive style, motivation, abilities, and context as predictors of executives' creative performance. *Creativity and Innovation Management, 8*(3), 188-196.

Fowler, F. J. (1993) *Survey research methods* (2nd ed.). Newbury Park, Ca: Sage.

Gall, M. D., Borg, W. R., & Gall, J. P. (1996). *Educational research: An introduction* (6th ed.). New York: Longman.

Gaziel, H. (1993). *Coping with occupational stress among teachers: A cross-cultural study, 29*(1), p. 67.

Goorian, B. (2000). *Alternative teacher compensation.* (Report No. ED-EA-00-08). Eugene, OR: Office of Educational Research and Improvement. (ERIC Documentation Reproductive Service No. ED 446368)

Guskey, T. R. (1985). Staff development and teacher change. *Educational Leadership, 42*(7), 57-60.

Guskey, T. R. (2000). *Evaluating professional development.* Thousand Oaks, CA: Corwin Press.

Hammond, G. & Onikama, D. (1997). *At risk teachers.* (Report No. SP 039 328). Honolulu, HI: Pacific Resources for Education and Learning. (ERIC Document Reproduction Service No. ED442796)

Harris, A. (2003). Teacher leadership as distributed leadership: Heresy, fantasy, or possibility? *School Leadership and Management, 23,* 3.

Hein, D. L. (1973). *An evaluation of the affective domain component of a teacher preparation project as measured by instruments using the affective domain continuum,* an unpublished doctoral dissertation. University of Northern Colorado.

Herzberg, F. (1959). *The motivation to work.* New York: John Wiley & Sons, Inc.

Herzberg, F. (1962). *Work and the nature of man.* New York: Thomas Y. Crowell Publishers.

Hess, F. (2004). Teacher quality, teacher pay. *Policy Review.*

Hesset, J. (1990). *Understanding Psychology.* New York: Random Press.

Ho, A. (2000). *A conceptual change approach to staff development: A model for program design.* Educational Development Unit. Hong Kong Polytechnic University, Hong Kong.

Hom, P. & Caranikis-Walker, F., Prussia, G., & Griffeth, R. (1992) A meta-analytical structural equations analysis of a model of employee turnover. *Journal of Applied Psychology, 77,* 890-909.

Hom, P. & Griffeth, R. (1995). *Employee turnover.* Cincinnati, OH: South-Western.

Hom, P. & Kinicki, A. (2001). Towards a greater understanding of how satisfaction drive employees turnover. *Academy of Management Journal, 44,* 975.

Houston Independent School District. (2004). Website. Retrieved April 7, 2004 from www.houstonisd.org

Houston Independent School District. (2005). Website. Retrieved March 10, 2005 from www.houstonisd.org

Howey, K. R. (1985). Six major functions of staff development: An expanded imperative. *Journal of Teacher Education, 36*(1), 58-64.

Hunter, B. M. (1989). *Teacher burnout and social support: An administrative perspective*. Unpublished doctoral of dissertation. University of Houston.

Huizinga, G. (1970). *Maslow's need hierarchy in the work situation.* Groningen, Netherlands: Wollters-Noordhoff Publishing.

Igbaria, M., Parasuraman, S., Badawy, M. K., (1994, June). Work experiences, job involvement, and quality of work like among information systems personnel. *IS Job Involvement,* 175-201.

Ingersoll, R. M. (1999). *Teacher turnover, teacher shortage, and the organization of schools.* A CTP Working Paper.

Jansen, J. (995). Effective schools? *Comparative Education, 31*(2) 181-201.

Janssen, O. (2003). Innovative behavior and job involvement at the price of conflict and less satisfactory relations with co-workers. *Journal of Occupational and Organizational Psychology, 76*, 347-364.

Johnston, M. W., Griffeth, R., Burton, S., & Carson, P. P. (1993). An exploratory investigation into the relationships between promotion and turnover: A quasi-experimental longitudinal study. *Journal of Management, 19*(1), 33-49.

Johnson, S. M. (1998, April). Telling all sides of the truth. *Educational Leadership,* 12-16.

Johnson, S. M. (2001, January). Can professional certification for teachers reshape teaching as a career? *Phi Delta Kappan,* 393-399.

Johnson, S. M., & Kardos, S. (2002, March). Keeping new teachers in mind. *Educational Leadership, 59,* 12-16.

Johnson, S. M., & Landman, J. (2000). "Sometimes bureaucracy has its charms" : The working conditions of teachers in deregulated schools. *Teacher College Record, 102*(1), 85-124.

Johnson, S. M., Kaufmann, D., Kardos, S. M., Liu, E., & Peske, H. G. (2001, December). The next generation of teachers; Changing conceptions of a career in teaching. *Phi Delta Kappan,* 304-311.

Jones, J. S., and J. Lowe. (1990). Changing teacher behavior: Effective staff development. *Adult Learning I* (7), 8-10.

Kelley, C. (1995). *Teacher compensation and organization.* (Report No. TM520125) Madison WI: Consortium for Research in Education. (ERIC Documentation Reproductive Service No. EJ 545438)

Kelley, C., & Odden, A. (1995). *Reinventing teacher compensation systems.* (Report No. EA 027106). Madison, WI: Consortium for Research in Education. (ERIC Documentation Reproductive Service No. ED 3870910)

Kelley, C. & Odden, A. & (2000). *Addressing teacher quality and supply through compensation policy.* Education Finance Research Consortium. Symposium on the Teacher Workforce. University of Wisconsin-Madison.

Kelley, C., Odden, A., Milanowski, A., Heneman, H. III, (2000). *School-based performance award programs, teacher motivation, and school performance: Finding from a study of three program.* (Report No. CPRE-RR-R308A600003) Philadelphia, PA: Consortium for Policy Research in Education. (ERIC Document Reproduction Service No. EA 032559)

Kelley, C., Odden, A., Milanowski, A., Heneman, H. III, (2000). *The motivational effects of school based performance.* (Report No. RB-29-Febraury 2000). Philadelphia, PA: Consortium for Policy Research in Education. (ERIC Document Reproduction Service No. ED 440473)

Kershaw, A. (1995). *Teacher's assessment of the agenda and the organization of staff development programs as suggested in current research* (Report No. SP 035-639). Illinois: Teacher and Teaching Education. (ERIC Document Reproduction Service No. ED 379210)

Lafee, S. (2003). Professional learning communities. *School Administrator, 60*(5), 6-13.

Lambert, L. (1989). The end of an era of staff development. *Educational Leadership, 47*(1), 78-81.

Lambert, L. (2002). A framework for shared leadership. *Educational Leadership,* 37-40.

Lauro, D. R. Jr., (1995). Five approaches to professional development compared. *T.H.E. Journal, 22*(10), 61-65.

Lawler, E. E. III (1973). *Motivation in work organizations.* Monterey, CA: Brooks/Cole.

Lawler, E. E. III (1986). *High-involvement management.* San Francisco, CA: Jossey Bass Publishers.

Lawler, E. E. III, Mohrman, S. A., & Ledford, G. E. (1995). *Creating high performance organizations.* San Francisco, CA: Jossey Bass Publishers.

Leach, D. J., Wall, T. D., Jackson, P. R., (2003). The effect of empowerment on job knowledge: An empirical test involving operators of complex technology. *Journal of Occupational Organizational Psychology, 76,* 27-52.

Leonard, P. & Leonard, L. (2001). The collaborative prescription: Remedy or reverie? *International Journal of Education, 4*(4) 383-399.

Locke, E. A. (1969). What is job satisfaction? *Organization Behavioral and Human Performance, 4,* 309-36.

Magestro, P., Stanford-Blair, N. (2000). A tool for meaningful staff development. *Educational Leadership, 57,* 34-5.

Ma, X. & MacMillan, R. (1999, Sep/Oct). Influence of workplace conditions on teachers' job satisfaction. *Journal of Educational Research, 99*(1), 9.

Maehr, M. (Eds.), (1984). *Meaning and motivation: Toward a theory of personal investment,* (vol. 1). San Diego: Academic Press.

Maslow, A. H. (1954). *Motivation and personality.* New York: Harper.

McClelland, D. (1975). *Power: The inner experience.* New York: Penguin Books Ltd.

Merkle, L. A. (1997). *Factor analysis of the self-motivation inventory.* Unpublished doctoral dissertation, University of Houston.

Merriam-Webster. (2005). Website. Retrieved January 27, 2003 from http://www.m-w.com/home.htm

Moreira, H., Fox, K. R., & Sparkes, A. C. (2002). Job motivation profiles of physical educators: theoretical background and instrument development. *British Educational Research Journal, 28*(6), 845-861.

Mohrman, Wohlstetter, et al. (1994). *School based management.* San Francisco, CA: Jossey Bass Publishers.

Mulford, B. & Silins, H. (2003). Leadership for organizational learning and improve student outcomes-what do know? *Cambridge Journal of Education, 33*(2), 175-195.

National Council States on In-service Education. (1980). *Providing leadership for staff development and in-service education,* November 1979 (No. 371.1). Syracuse, NY.

NSDC Standards for staff development. Retrieved February 6, 2002, from wysiwyg://108/http://www.nsdc.org/list.htm & http://www.nsdc.org/library/standards2001.html

Odden, A. (1995). *Incentive, school organization, and teacher compensation.* (Report No. EA 026609). Madison WI: Consortium for Research in Education. (ERIC Documentation Reproductive Service No. ED 380896)

Orlich, D. C. (1989). *Staff development: enhancing human potential.* Boston, MA: Allyn and Bacon.

Parkay, F. W. & Hoover, N. L. (1986). *A self-assessment procedure for motivating personnel to use school and teacher effectiveness research.* (Report No. EA 020-313). San Francisco, CA: America Educational Research Association. (ERIC Document Reproduction Service ED 301923)

Paul, R. J., Niehoff, B. P., & Turnley, W H. (2000). Empowerment, expectations, and the psychological contract – Managing the dilemmas and gaining the advantages. *Journal of Socio-Economic, 29*(5), 13.

Penner, Janet S. (1999). *Teacher and principal perceptions of factors influencing teachers' decisions to participate in professional development activities.* Unpublished doctoral dissertation, University of Houston.

Professional development today. (1995). Retrieved February 6, 2002, from http://www.ed.gov/pubs/CPRE/t61/t61c.html.

Purcell, L. (1987). *Staff development.* (Report No. EA 019627) Georgia: Educational Management. (ERIC Document Reproduction Service ED 286258)

Pun, K. P., Chin, K. S., & Gill, R. (2001). Determinants of employee involvement. *Total Quality Management, 12*(1), 95-109.

Ramsden, P. (1992). *Learning to teach in higher education.* London: Routledge.

Reyes, P., & Shin, H. (1995). Teacher commitment and job satisfaction: A causal analysis. *Journal of School Leadership, 5,* 22-39.

Riipinen, M. (1997). The relationship between job involvement and well-being. *The Journal of Psychology, 13*(1), 81-89.

Rosenholtz, S. J. 1991). *Teachers' workplace: The organizations of schools.* New York: Teachers College Press.

Rubin, L. J. (1978). *Some postulations and principals on the continuing professional education of teachers*. In L. Rubin (Ed.). The in-service education of teachers: Trends, processes, and prescriptions Boston: Allyn and Bacon. 22-306.

Runyan, C. K. (1991, November). *Empowering beginning teachers though developmental induction*. The Annual Conference of the National Council of States on In-service Education. Houston, Texas.

Russell, J. J. (1992). *Theory into practice: The realities of shared decision making*. Unpublished doctoral dissertation, Fordham University.

Ryan, L. (1987). *The complete in-service staff development program: A step-by-step manual for school administrators*. Englewood Cliff, New Jersey: Prentice Hall.

Schambier, R. F. (1983). *Staff development: The carrot or the stick?* (Report No. CE 037 532). Philadelphia, PA: American Association for Adult and Continuing Education. (ERIC Document Reproduction Service ED 237658).

Scott, K. D. & Wimbush J. (1991). Teacher absenteeism in secondary education. *Educational Administration Quarterly, 27*(4), 506-529.

Shann, M. (2001, Nov/Dec). Professional commitment and satisfaction among teachers in urban middle schools. *Journal of Educational Research, 98*(92), 2, pp. 7.

Shapiro, G. (2000). Employee involvement: Opening the diversity Pandora's box? *Personnel Review, 29*(3), 304-323.

Silver, P. (1982, April). Synthesis of research on teacher motivation. *Research Information Services,* 551-554.

Sjöberg, A., & Sverke, M. (2000). The interactive effect of job involvement and organizational commitment on job turnover revisited: A note on the mediating role of turnover intention. *Scandinavian Journal of Psychology, 41*, 247-252.

Solo, L. J. (1985). School site staff development: Structures and processes. *Education and Urban Society*, 17(3), 332-340.

Sparks, D. & Hirsh, S. (1999). A national plan for improving professional development. Retrieved February 6, 2002, from http://www.nsdc.org/library/NSDCPlan.html

Speck, M. & Knipe, C. (2001). *Why can't we get it right? Professional development in our schools*. Thousand Oaks, CA: Corwin Press, Inc.

Spector, P.E. (1997). *Job satisfaction: Application, assessment causes, and consequence*. Thousand Oaks, CA: Sage.

Spillane, J. P. (1999). External reform initiatives and teachers' effort to reconstruct their practice: The mediating role of teachers' zone of enactment. *J. Curriculum Studies, 31*, 143-175.

Spillane, J. P., Halverson, R., & Diamond, J. B. (2004). Towards a theory of leadership practice: A distributed perspective. *J. Curriculum Studies, 36*(1), 3-34.

SPSS Student Version 12.0 for Windows (2003). Prentice-Hall. A Pearson Company.

Strahan, D. (2002). Promoting a collaborative professional culture in three elementary schools that have beaten the odds. *The Elementary School Journal,* 104(2).

Talbert, T. (2003, Summer). Come to the edge: Embracing teacher empowerment for the 21st century. *Action in Teacher Education, 25*(2), 51-55.

Texas Education Agency (2005). Website. Retrieved March 8, 2005, from http://www.tea.state.tx.us/

Thompson, J., & Cooley, V. E. (1984). Improvement in leadership, curriculum, and staff development can end to long-term gains. *NASSP Bulletin, 68* (476), 1-6.

Townsend, M. L. (1992). *Moving toward clearer concepts of burnout and exhaustion: The construction and testing of social types of teachers.* Unpublished master's thesis, University of Houston.

Turbowitz, S. & Longo, P. (1997). *How it works - Inside a school - college collaboration.* New York: Teachers College Press.

Tyack, D. (1993). Constructing difference: Historical reflections on schooling and social diversity. *Teacher College Record, 95*, 8-34.

Tyler, R. W. (1971). First report from the national assessment. *Educational Leadership, 28*(6), 577-80.

U.S. Department of Education (2005). Website. Retrieved February 28, 2005 from http://www.ed.gov/.

U.S. Department of Labor (2002). Website. Retrieved April 7, 2002 from www.dol.gov/dol/pwba.

What is the national staff development council? (2001). Website. Retrieved February 6, 2002 from http://www.nsdc.org/educatorcontent.htm

Webster's New Collegiate Dictionary (1988).

Wilson, S. & Coolican, M. J. (1996). How high and low self empowered teachers work with colleagues and school principals. *Journal of Educational Theory, 30,* 99-117.

Wu V. & Short, P. (1996, March) The relationship of empowerment to teacher job commitment and job satisfaction. *The Journal of Instructional Psychology, 23,* 85-99.

Van Knippenberg, D. (2000). Work motivation and performance: A social identity perspective. *Applied Psychology, 49*(3), 357-371.

Zeichner, K. & Klehr, M. (1999). *Teacher research as professional development for P-12 educators.* (Report No. SP 039 685). Washington, DC: National Partnership for Excellence and Accountability in Teaching. (ERIC Documentation Reproductive Service ED 448156)

Zigarelli, M., (1996). An Empirical Test of Conclusion from Effective Schools Research. *The Journal of Educational Research, 92,* 2.

Appendix A

Teacher Data Questionnaire

Teacher Data Questionnaire

Please respond to the following items.

Sex

Male _____   Female _____

Ethnicity

Asian _____   African American _____   Hispanic _____

White _____   Other, please specify _____

Age

_____

Years of teaching experience.

_____ years

Years at your current school.

_____ Years

At how many schools have you taught?

_____ Schools

What grade level(s) are you teaching this year?

_____

Will you receive a Stipend this year?

_____

Highest Degree Earned

Bachelors _____   Master's _____   Doctorate _____

Appendix B

Consent Form

Appendix C

Follow-up Letter

Dear Sir or Madame,

As a teacher, your perceptions of the issues in education are very important. Although you have many tasks to complete, I hope you had the time to complete the survey placed in you box earlier this week. If you have already returned your survey to the collection box in the front office of your school, please disregard this email, only one survey set is needed from each participant. If you have not returned your survey, please do so at your earliest convenience. Your participation is greatly appreciated and may provide improvements to the field of education.

Sincerely

J. deValentino

www.ingramcontent.com/pod-product-compliance
Lightning Source LLC
Chambersburg PA
CBHW081011040426

42443CB00016B/3487